*David S. Yost*

# The US and Nuclear Deterrence in Europe

*Adelphi Paper* 326

Oxford University Press, Great Clarendon Street, Oxford ox2 6DP
Oxford New York
Athens Auckland Bangkok Bombay Calcutta Cape Town
Dar es Salaam Delhi Florence Hong Kong Istanbul Karachi
Kuala Lumpur Madras Madrid Melbourne Mexico City
Nairobi Paris Singapore Taipei Tokyo Toronto
and associated companies in
Berlin Ibadan

Oxford is a trade mark of Oxford University Press

Published in the United States
by Oxford University Press Inc., New York

© International Institute for Strategic Studies 1999

**First published** March 1999 by **Oxford University Press** for
**International Institute for Strategic Studies**
23 Tavistock Street, London WC2E 7NQ

**Director** John Chipman
**Editor** Gerald Segal
**Assistant Editor** Matthew Foley
**Design and Production** Mark Taylor

British Library Cataloguing in Publication Data
Data available

Library of Congress Cataloguing in Publication Data

**ISBN** 0-19-922426-9
**ISSN** 0567-932X

*contents*

| | |
|---|---|
| ABM | Anti-Ballistic Missile Treaty |
| ACM | advanced cruise missile |
| ALCM | air-launched cruise missile |
| CDU | Christian Democratic Union (Germany) |
| CFSP | Common Foreign and Security Policy |
| CIA | Central Intelligence Agency (US) |
| CTBT | Comprehensive Test Ban Treaty |
| CTR | Cooperative Threat Reduction programme |
| EU | European Union |
| G-8 | Group of Eight industrial nations |
| ICBM | intercontinental ballistic missile |
| ICJ | International Court of Justice |
| INF | Intermediate-range Nuclear Forces Treaty |
| IRBM | intermediate-range ballistic missile |
| NAC | North Atlantic Council (NATO) |
| NGO | non-governmental organisation |
| NMD | national missile defence |
| NPG | Nuclear Planning Group |
| NPT | Non-Proliferation Treaty |
| NSA | negative security assurance |
| NSC | National Security Council (US) |
| NSNF | non-strategic nuclear forces |

Nuclear issues have gained surprising prominence in NATO's deliberations about a new Strategic Concept since early 1998. The adoption of the new Concept at the Washington Summit in April 1999 will not, however, resolve the debates about the future of US nuclear forces and commitments in Europe. Events since the Alliance's Strategic Concept review began, in Russia and further afield, have underscored how the context for these forces and commitments may undergo unpredictable changes. Continued uncertainties about Russia's future have bolstered arguments for upholding NATO's established nuclear policies. Positive political trends and nuclear-force reductions in Russia could yet lead the US and its Allies to make further adjustments in their nuclear policies. But the US nuclear guarantee remains a crucial part of NATO's ability to play an important role in international security, both within and beyond Europe.

Russia's instability has been the most important factor shaping attitudes in the US and NATO as a whole. Even with a smaller arsenal than at present, Russia is still likely to remain a risky strategic unknown well into the future. The Indian and Pakistani nuclear-weapon tests in May 1998 have also led some observers to forecast a fundamental erosion of the nuclear non-proliferation regime, with the likelihood that new nuclear powers will emerge. India and Pakistan may choose to adhere to the Comprehensive Test Ban Treaty (CTBT), participate in the fissile-material production cut-off negotiations, and take other measures that could limit the damage to the non-proliferation regime. But the basic strategic reality is that there are now seven declared nuclear powers, where once there were five.

NATO's nuclear posture and supporting policy rationales have inherent merits in the eyes of Alliance governments. Essentially, these are:

- US nuclear forces in Europe send a more potent deterrent message about US commitments than would be the case if the Alliance relied solely on US weapons at sea and in North America.

- If US nuclear commitments were not made visible, potential adversaries could more easily convince themselves that the Americans would not take nuclear risks to defend their Allies and interests in Europe.

- Without the nuclear presence in Europe, the Americans themselves might not take their nuclear promises as seriously; it would be easier for the US to distance itself from a crisis and decide not to honour its nuclear commitments.

- The US nuclear presence ensures extensive European participation in nuclear roles, as well as consultative arrangements for multinational nuclear policy. Without this participation, the Alliance's confidence in its strength and cohesion would be weaker, as would be its confidence in the probable perception of its resolve and capabilities by adversaries.

## The Requirements of Extended Deterrence

US nuclear forces in Europe have a long and complex history. The earliest strategic documents of the Atlantic Alliance make clear that, from the outset, the US and its Allies understood US security commitments as including nuclear protection against coercion or aggression.[1] Much of the subsequent history of the Alliance has been marked by debates over the meaning of US nuclear 'guarantees' – above all, the requirements of what came to be known as extended deterrence. During the Cold War, NATO Europe's leaders generally agreed that a US nuclear presence on the ground was one of the requirements for credible extended deterrence. This judgment remains widely shared among the politicians, officials and experts in NATO's European countries who take an active part in defence and security affairs.

Large-scale reductions in US nuclear forces in Europe nonetheless began in the late 1970s, and were boosted by the 1987 Intermediate-range Nuclear Forces (INF) Treaty prohibiting US and Soviet land-based missiles with ranges of 500–5,500 kilometres. In September and October 1991, the US and NATO decided to remove all ground-launched systems. From Cold War peaks of about 7,000 US weapons, unconfirmed published reports have put the number of remaining weapons at between 480 and 700 gravity bombs for US and allied aircraft in Europe.[2] Seven European Allies (Belgium, Germany, Greece, Italy, the Netherlands, Turkey and the UK) provide delivery systems for US nuclear warheads and 'host nation facilities for United States nuclear capable forces'.[3] The central importance of the nuclear presence was reaffirmed in the Alliance's Strategic Concept, approved in November 1991:

> *A credible Alliance nuclear posture and the demonstration of Alliance solidarity and common commitment to war prevention continue to require widespread participation by European Allies involved in collective defence planning in nuclear roles, in peacetime basing of nuclear forces on their territory and in command, control and consultation arrangements. Nuclear forces based in Europe and committed to NATO provide an essential political and military link between the European and the North American members of the Alliance.[4]*

US nuclear commitments to NATO have not substantially changed. All the Allies have continued to uphold the importance of nuclear deterrence in their periodic communiqués, and US extended deterrence in Europe has remained a multilateral Alliance process. This ensures that some non-nuclear Allies have direct responsibilities, accepting nuclear weapons on their territory and (in wartime) delivering them. Moreover, non-nuclear Allies without such responsibilities also contribute to the development of Alliance policy and strategy. Since the founding of the Nuclear Planning

**Table I** *NATO Sub-strategic Nuclear-Force Reductions, 1971–1993*

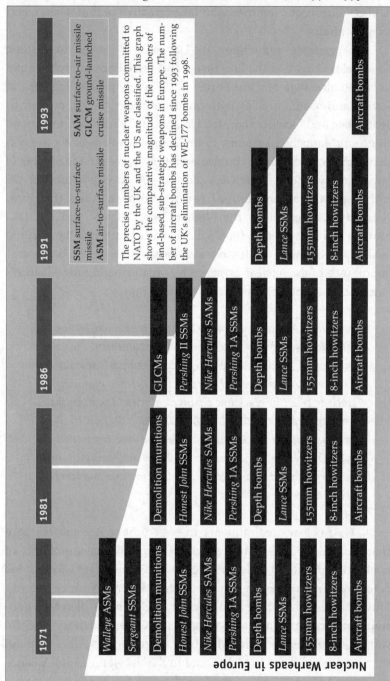

The precise numbers of nuclear weapons committed to NATO by the UK and the US are classified. This graph shows the comparative magnitude of the numbers of land-based sub-strategic weapons in Europe. The number of aircraft bombs has declined since 1993 following the UK's elimination of WE-177 bombs in 1998.

SSM surface-to-surface missile
ASM air-to-surface missile
SAM surface-to-air missile
GLCM ground-launched cruise missile

**Source** *NATO Basic Fact Sheet No. 27*, NATO Office of Information and Press, January 1998

Group (NPG) in 1966–67, the NATO nuclear-consultation process has cultivated patterns of cooperation which are highly valued by the participants.

Throughout the history of the Alliance, US nuclear forces have been seen as supremely important political instruments; their fundamental purpose has been deterrence and war-prevention. However, several important questions about extended deterrence and limited nuclear options were never fully answered during the Cold War. These include the extent to which using theatre nuclear forces would imply linkage or 'coupling' to US intercontinental forces, and how escalation to higher levels of nuclear violence could be controlled.[5]

Despite uncertainties about the requirements of extended deterrence, three closely linked rationales for the US nuclear presence in Europe have traditionally been offered.

- First, these weapons enhance the credibility of US extended-deterrence guarantees in a way that sole reliance on forces at sea and in North America would not. They connect US security commitments to the country's intercontinental nuclear forces, thus making visible the 'transatlantic link' for protection in accordance with Article 5 of the North Atlantic Treaty.
- Second, multinational decision-making and policy implementation promote the Alliance's political cohesion. The US nuclear presence has increased the political influence of the non-nuclear European Allies regarding US nuclear policy, because they have accepted nuclear roles and responsibilities.
- Third, US nuclear weapons in Europe, together with the rest of the US nuclear posture, underpin America's broader role in international politics.

This paper assesses the prospects for US nuclear forces and commitments in Europe in the next ten to 15 years, and surveys the most important factors likely to influence America's nuclear posture. These factors differ in their nature and significance, and cannot be considered in isolation. The likelihood of additional Russian nuclear arms-control proposals, for example, must be seen in the context of

NATO enlargement. Similarly, ostensibly minor adjustments in the US nuclear posture, championed by some in the interests of non-proliferation, could have far-reaching political and strategic consequences in Europe.

## chapter 1

# Russia and NATO Enlargement

Historically, US nuclear forces have been seen as necessary to counter-balance the military capabilities of the Soviet Union and, since 1991, of Russia. According to NATO's Strategic Concept of 1991, one of the Alliance's four 'fundamental security tasks' is to 'preserve the strategic balance within Europe'.[1] The document adds that 'Even in a non-adversarial and co-operative relationship, Soviet military capability and build-up potential, including its nuclear dimension, still constitute the most significant factor of which the Alliance has to take account'.[2] The document notes, moreover, that the 'supreme guarantee of the security of the Allies is provided by the strategic nuclear forces of the Alliance, particularly those of the United States', and that 'adequate sub-strategic forces based in Europe ... will provide an essential link with strategic nuclear forces, reinforcing the trans-Atlantic link'.[3]

US nuclear weapons in Europe help to convince Moscow that Washington's security commitments are genuine, thereby encouraging caution and reducing the risk of Russian adventurism. Moscow has evidently always regarded the US nuclear presence in Europe with great seriousness. It was one of the main targets of Soviet diplomacy in Europe from the early 1950s. Since 1991, the Russians have repeatedly expressed their interest in seeing US nuclear forces removed. NATO governments generally agree that, despite Russia's setbacks in Chechnya and its other problems, the country's military capabilities (especially its nuclear arms) could in certain circumstances still pose significant threats to Western security interests. NATO therefore requires an effective nuclear posture to ensure stability and balance in its relations with Russia.

Western analyses hold that the US military and nuclear presence in NATO Europe actually serves Russian security interests by helping to discourage the renationalisation of defence policies, nuclear proliferation and the formation of new competitive coalitions. It is likely that some Russian politicians and analysts understand and appreciate the merits of this argument. However,

*Russia could still threaten NATO's strategic interests*

acknowledging that NATO and the US military and nuclear presence in Europe benefit Russian security would be neither popular nor career-enhancing, either for a politician or an international-affairs analyst.

Similarly, since the US is trying to cultivate cooperative relations with Russia, referring to the country as a potential nuclear threat is awkward. Officials have generally been circumspect in discussing the strategic and political functions of US nuclear forces *vis-à-vis* Russia. However, at the September 1994 press conference announcing the results of the Nuclear Posture Review – which confirmed that US nuclear forces in Europe would be retained – then Deputy Secretary of Defense John Deutch remarked:

> Let me remind you that Russia has little prospect of returning to the kind of conventional force structure that they had at the height of the Cold War due to the collapse of their economy and the change in their political situation. It is a less expensive and less demanding matter for them to return to a much more aggressive nuclear posture. If something does go wrong in Russia, it is likely that it is in the nuclear forces area that we will face the first challenge.[4]

## Changes in Russian Security Policy

Russia's nuclear forces are one of its few remaining justifications for claiming great-power status. Even under President Boris Yeltsin and others viewed in the West as reformers, Russian strategy is placing increased emphasis on nuclear weapons for several reasons. These include the demise of the Warsaw Pact, the Soviet Union's collapse and Russia's declining conventional capabilities. For large-scale contingencies, at least in the short term, nuclear arms are likely to appear a more effective and readily available form of military power than the country's conventional forces.

Problems affecting all branches of the military include inadequate and unpaid salaries; deficiencies in food, clothing and housing, even for officers; under-funded and insufficient training and maintenance; and, above all, a dramatic ebb in status, morale, cohesion and discipline, with growing evidence of crime and corruption.[5] It is therefore not surprising that some Russian discussions of military doctrine tend to see nuclear weapons as a substitute for the high-technology conventional systems demon-strated by the US in the 1990–91 Gulf War. Many of these capabilities are, for the foreseeable future, beyond Russia's economic grasp.

Russia's draft military doctrine of 1992 foresaw the possible abandonment of the 1982 Soviet no-first-use pledge. This policy change was confirmed in November 1993, when the new doctrine was officially promulgated. The no-first-use pledge appears in retrospect to have been bogus, and aimed mainly at Western public opinion.[6] It seems to have been abandoned for various reasons, and only partly because it was premised on Soviet conventional superiority. Some high-level Soviet military officers apparently never endorsed it. In May 1992, Colonel-General Igor Rodionov, then head of the General Staff Academy, argued that 'Statements about "no first use of nuclear weapons", "retaliatory strikes", and "defensive character" indicate a repetition of the mistakes of past years – which stemmed from the self-advertisement of political leaders and irreparably damaged our defence'.[7] Rodionov was Russia's Minister of Defence from July 1996 to May 1997, when he was replaced by Igor Sergeyev, the head of the Strategic Rocket Forces.

The national-security concept approved by Yeltsin in December 1997 notes that nuclear deterrence may prevent 'both nuclear and conventional large-scale or regional wars'. It also stated that 'the virtual absence of the threat of large-scale aggression against Russia while its nuclear deterrent potential is preserved makes it possible to redistribute the resources of the state and society to resolve acute domestic problems on a priority basis'.[8] In August 1998, Yeltsin signed a similar document reaffirming the role of nuclear deterrence in reducing the risk of large-scale conflict.[9] In

1997, senior officials such as then Foreign Minister Yevgeny
Primakov and Secretary of the Russian Federation Security Council
Ivan Rybkin restated Russia's readiness to use nuclear arms in
response to aggression by conventional means. Many Russian
military authors have discussed limited-use options for purposes
such as averting defeat, stabilising
the line held by Russian forces, 'de-
escalating' military conflict and
preventing a geographical extension
of fighting.[10] These doctrinal statements and the weaknesses of
Russia's conventional forces imply that the country's threshold for
nuclear-weapons use may have been lowered.

> *Russia may have lowered
> the 'nuclear threshold'*

Doctrinal affirmations of the validity of nuclear deterrence –
and, in certain contingencies, of limited nuclear operations – have
been accompanied by the pursuit of new nuclear-delivery systems.
The US has had no development programmes for new systems since
1992. In contrast, Russia has been developing a new single-warhead
intercontinental ballistic missile (ICBM), the SS-X-27 or *Topol*-M, and
a new submarine-launched ballistic missile (SLBM), the SS-NX-28.
Officials have also discussed the potential advantages of new types
of nuclear weapons.[11] Some Russians have expressed interest in
developing nuclear weapons with limited collateral effects, partly in
order to minimise radioactive contamination.[12] The CTBT's restric-
tions would hamper the development of such weapons unless
Russia chose to evade the Treaty's limited verification regime. It
could, for example, conceal low-yield tests in large underground
chambers. According to some accounts, in January 1996 Russia may
have conducted a low-yield test 'in a way that would not leave a
seismic signature'.[13]

A great deal of press commentary has focused on the delays in
Russian ratification of the Strategic Arms Reduction Talks (START) II
Treaty. However, significant problems have also arisen in
implementing US–Russian presidential understandings relating to
nuclear arms. Russia has apparently done less than the US to fulfil
the commitments made in 1991 and 1992 concerning eliminating
certain types of non-strategic nuclear weapons. It has also been
comparatively uninformative about its activities in this area. The
dialogue on nuclear weapons in the NATO–Russia Permanent Joint
Council (PJC), established in May 1997, has thrown little light on this

subject. In May 1998, it was reported that 'At a recent meeting to exchange information on tactical nuclear weapons, the Russian delegation's presentation was "extremely fuzzy" and failed to provide any illumination on the fate of some 10,000 to 12,000 of its tactical nuclear weapons, according to NATO participants'.[14]

Yeltsin's statements on 27 May 1997 that Russian nuclear weapons are no longer targeted on NATO countries have yet to be clarified. Nothing has apparently been added to what Russian commentators declared at the time: that what Yeltsin 'meant to say was that Russia would stop the permanent targetting of missiles against the West – which would not prevent Russia launching a rapid atomic strike if it wanted'.[15] The reciprocal inspections and data exchanges that President Bill Clinton and Yeltsin agreed in May 1995 have not been implemented, and other US–Russian agreements in this area have not been fully carried out.[16] Nonetheless, the US-funded Cooperative Threat Reduction (CTR) programme has made limited progress in the protection, control and accounting of warheads in Russia.

Some Russian analysts have argued that the country's conventional military weakness could lead to the operational use of nuclear weapons, notably in crises on its periphery. Paul Felgen-gauer, a Russian journalist specialising in international security affairs, observed during the Chechen conflict of 1994–96 that:

> The Russian Army could easily suffer defeat in a local conflict in the Caucasus or in Central Asia. The political and military consequences of such a defeat could prove wholly unacceptable to Russia, and a direct threat to use nuclear weapons or even a limited 'demonstration' nuclear strike could for this reason suddenly become the last realistic possibility of winning or evening up a war that has been lost, although no one in Moscow is seriously planning such actions at this time, of course.[17]

The risk of such nuclear use – perhaps by officers acting without Moscow's full authorisation – may be higher than is generally suspected, in view of reports about the primitive character of some Russian technical security measures.[18] In conjunction with other policy instruments, US nuclear forces in Europe might help to dissuade Russians from resorting to nuclear weapons in desperation. Depending on the circumstances of such a crisis, the US and the rest of the Alliance would probably be determined to contain the conflict and prevent escalation to higher levels of violence, to restore the security and integrity of the NATO area and to ensure against any recurrence of nuclear-weapons use if efforts to deter it had failed.

## Alternative Political Directions in Russia

Whether Russia might actually threaten NATO will depend largely on the course of the country's politics. Four possible political futures in Russia merit attention. The first is democratisation, economic liberalisation and cooperation with the West. This would imply building on various activities, including those associated with arms-control agreements, the CTR programme, Russian participation in the NATO-led Stabilisation Force (SFOR) in Bosnia-Herzegovina and the NATO–Russia PJC. Evidence of sustained democratisation and cooperation in dealing with international security problems could eventually undermine those grounds for retaining the US nuclear presence in Europe which are based on insuring against potential Russian coercion or aggression.

A second possible direction for Russia – a unified dictatorship and confrontation with the West – would in some ways represent a return to the situation that prevailed during the Cold War. NATO governments would probably support maintaining the US nuclear presence in Europe. NATO would then face traditional conundrums, such as 'how much is enough?'. It is unclear whether an anti-Western Russia led by a nationalist dictatorship would follow the same deterrent logic and 'rules of the road' observed by the Soviet Politburo. The legitimising ideology and economic and geostrategic circumstances of a new Russian dictatorship would probably differ substantially from those of the Soviet Union. Sergey Rogov, the Director of Russia's USA and Canada Institute, has compared today's Russia with Germany's Weimar Republic, adding that there are 'strong internal forces pushing Russia into "self-isolation" as a disgruntled nation seeking to undermine the international order … with a "more assertive" stance toward protecting what are seen as Russia's national interests'.[19] Even if the Russians could muster the resources to exert greater influence in former imperial domains, doing so might only increase Western political unity and resolve to resist Russian expansionism. It could make the Alliance more determined to maintain its military posture, including US nuclear forces in Europe, in good order.

Russian politicians have repeatedly raised a third possible direction – civil war, regionalisation and confrontation with the West. In January 1997, General Lev Rokhlin, at the time chairman of the Duma's Defence Committee, warned that the 'disintegration of Russia itself' could be imminent, in part due to regional separatism and the problems of maintaining a unified national army. These developments could, Rokhlin feared, lead to intervention in Russia by foreign powers.[20] Deborah Yarsike Ball's 1995 survey of Russian military officers found that 'in four of the nine regions containing nuclear weapons ... the majority of the officers openly stated they would disobey orders to put down a separatist rebellion ... Moscow could lose control because regional authorities need only the passivity of the military to win such a showdown'.[21] According to reports published in October 1996, a US Central Intelligence Agency (CIA) analysis had concluded that:

> *under normal circumstances, the prospect of an unauthor-*
> *ized nuclear-missile launch or a blackmail attempt using*
> *nuclear arms is low, despite continuing turmoil, political*
> *uncertainty and disarray in the armed forces ... A severe*
> *political crisis, however, could exacerbate existing dissension*
> *and factionalization in the military, possibly heightening*
> *tensions between Russian political and military leaders and*
> *even splitting the general staff of nuclear commands.*[22]

The implications for the US nuclear presence in Europe in these circumstances could depend on how events unfolded. It nonetheless seems likely that many of the Allies would judge it prudent to retain US nuclear forces in Europe as a hedge against the unknown.

In the fourth possible outcome, ambiguity, inconsistency and ambivalent relations with the West would persist. This would amount to a continuation of the situation since 1993: a nominally democratic regime pursuing erratic and contradictory policies, partly because of power-struggles within the government and within the country as a whole. According to Vladimir Shlapentokh, a prominent specialist in Russian affairs, 'in the next few years, and possibly even longer … Russia will continue to be a country with a stagnant economy, extremely high social polarization of the population, and permanent internal political conflicts'.[23] Maintaining the current Alliance nuclear posture is prudent given the risk that this fourth outcome could lead to domestic disorder and increasingly anti-Western policies.

## Russia and NATO Enlargement

The Allies have made it clear that they see no need to deploy US nuclear weapons in Eastern Europe. According to the Alliance's September 1995 *Study on NATO Enlargement*:

> *The coverage provided by Article 5, including its nuclear component, will apply to new members. There is no a priori requirement for the stationing of nuclear weapons on the territory of new members. In light of both the current international environment and the potential threats facing the Alliance, NATO's current nuclear posture will, for the foreseeable future, continue to meet the requirements of an enlarged Alliance. There is, therefore, no need now to change or modify any aspect of NATO's nuclear posture or policy, but the longer term implications of enlargement for both will continue to be evaluated. NATO should retain its existing nuclear capabilities along with its right to modify its nuclear posture as circumstances warrant.*[24]

The Alliance has never articulated the reasoning behind this policy, though financial and political factors probably entered into it. In addition, since several European Allies already provide facilities for US nuclear-capable forces, deployments across a broader geographic area were probably judged unnecessary for deterrence, despite the hypothetical advantages of more extensive participation in sharing roles and responsibilities.

NATO's position on this issue is sometimes referred to as the 'Three Nos' policy. In December 1996, the North Atlantic Council (NAC) declared that 'NATO countries have no intention, no plan, and no reason to deploy nuclear weapons on the territory of new members nor any need to change any aspect of NATO's nuclear posture or nuclear policy – and we do not foresee any future need to do so'.[25] The NATO–Russia Founding Act of May 1997, a political statement rather than a legally binding treaty, affirmed these points. It also added that NATO has 'no intention, no plan, and no reason to establish nuclear weapon storage sites' on the territory of new members.[26]

NATO's efforts to restate a clear and consistent policy in this regard have not eased Russian concerns. With the dissolution of the Warsaw Pact, Russia had to remove the nuclear weapons which the Soviet Union had placed on the territory of several East European states. Some Russians have argued that it is 'unfair' for the US to retain any nuclear presence in Europe. Some have asserted that the 1990 'Two Plus Four' Treaty on German unification, which ruled out deploying nuclear weapons on the territory of the former German Democratic Republic, established a precedent applicable to all former Warsaw Pact states. At the nuclear-safety summit in Moscow in April 1996, Yeltsin suggested a link between NATO expansion, the US *Russia's concerns about NATO expansion* nuclear presence in Europe and nuclear proliferation. Noting Russia's acquisition of the former-Soviet nuclear weapons in Belarus, Kazakstan and Ukraine (a process completed in 1996), Yeltsin stated that 'It is in our common interests to ensure that the nuclear weapons of all nuclear countries are also concentrated within the boundaries of their territories. Russia considers it a proliferation of nuclear arms when nuclear weapons are placed on the territory of non-nuclear states'.[27] This suggestion – together with Russian hints about the possible advantages of a nuclear-weapons-free zone from the Baltic to the Black Sea – could only have been aimed at the US nuclear weapons in Europe.

Other Russian officials also 'nuclearised' the dialogue over NATO enlargement. In February 1996, Viktor Mikhailov, then Minister of Atomic Energy, argued that if, for example, the Czech Republic joined NATO, nuclear weapons would 'one day' be deployed there. According to Mikhailov, 'since I am responsible for Russia's nuclear security, I have to take adequate measures. Very simple measures to make it so these sites don't exist. They will simply be destroyed'.[28] In July 1996, Primakov hinted that the Duma might insist that Russia withdraw from the INF Treaty and not ratify

START II unless arrangements were made forbidding any deployment of 'NATO's military infrastructure' on the territory of new allies.[29] In September 1996, Mikhailov added that NATO expansion could lead Russia to withdraw from the CTBT.[30]

Unofficial Russian sources took an even harder line. According to Anton Surikov, a close associate of Russian Communist Party leaders, NATO enlargement represents 'an attempt by Germany to resume its expansion ... through political and economic methods under the cover of the American "nuclear shield"'. For Surikov, 'the only possible solution lies in restraining NATO' by deploying nuclear weapons in Belarus, Kaliningrad, Crimea, Abkhazia, Georgia and Armenia, and on ships in the Baltic, Black and Barents seas. In Surikov's view, 'nobody intends to fight with Russia for the Baltic countries', owing in part to Russia's nuclear forces – 'one of the few convincing arguments for the West'.[31] He added that 'any attempt to bring the ... Baltic republics into NATO could create a serious international crisis' comparable with the 1962 Cuban missile crisis.[32] In 1996, Felgengauer reported that:

> *High-ranking officials of the Russian Defense Ministry by no means rule out the possibility that in response to, say, the integration of Poland into NATO's military structure, Moscow might deploy hundreds of tactical nuclear warheads in Kaliningrad Province, targeting them on Polish military and strategic facilities needed to support the operations of mobile attack forces.*[33]

Domestic political motives – such as appealing to the fears of nationalists – may be behind some of this Russian commentary. Statements implying that NATO would face a greater nuclear-weapon threat in the event of enlargement may also have amounted to posturing aimed at obtaining the best terms possible in collateral arrangements.

Ruling out future NATO deployments in a legal document, as some Russians proposed, would have foreclosed the Alliance's future security options without affecting Russian capabilities and options. It could also have helped to 'delegitimise' NATO's nuclear posture and set an undesirable precedent, probably without greatly reducing Russian hostility to enlargement. Alliance policy holds that new members will be full allies. They will not be 'second-class' associates in a nuclear-weapons-free zone without the rights and options open to other allies and, implicitly, without the full benefit of Article 5 protection. Formalising constraints on the future deployment of nuclear weapons in a legal document would have undermined the Alliance's cohesion and its sense of shared security and common purpose.

Russia's reactions to NATO enlargement, its enhanced doctrinal reliance on nuclear capabilities and uncertainties in its domestic politics have all reinforced the importance of maintaining US nuclear forces and commitments in Europe. The risks of setbacks for democratisation and reform in Russia are too serious for the Alliance to ignore.

## chapter 2

# WMD Proliferation

## Promoting Non-Proliferation within NATO

It is widely agreed that US nuclear weapons in Europe enhance the credibility of America's commitments to provide nuclear protection to its Allies. Withdrawing US nuclear forces might send a message of disengagement. It could lead to a renationalisation of defence policies, new alliances to compensate for the weakening or collapse of NATO and, perhaps in some cases, the pursuit of national nuclear-weapon programmes. The two most frequently cited examples in this regard are Germany and Turkey.

## Germany

In 1992, before he became Under-Secretary of Defense for Policy in the Clinton administration, Walter Slocombe wrote that 'A unified Germany would not readily rely indefinitely on a British or French deterrent. The practical issue, therefore, is whether there will be US nuclear weapons in Europe – or German ones'.[1] A survey of German military and civilian leaders in 1995 supports Slocombe's view. The sample was asked to estimate the degree of German interest in a national nuclear-weapon capability under various potential security conditions. Interest was extremely low when the posited future security environment included NATO and a US military and nuclear presence in Europe. In the absence of NATO and US military commitments, but with a European alliance in which Germany was aligned with the UK and France, interest increased, in part due to 'a

German hesitancy to trust the commitment of French or British guarantees of nuclear protection'. If the possible future security environment included no alliances and assumed that Germany would be alone in providing for its security, a high level of interest in a national nuclear-weapon programme was apparent.[2] Non-security

*arguments for a German nuclear identity*

incentives for acquiring a national capability included the prospect that nuclear weapons could 'contribute, at least indirectly, to new feelings of German pride, prestige, and sovereignty, as well as being credible instruments for international influence'. The survey found that non-security reasons increased as security ones grew. The survey's author, Major Mark Gose of the US Air Force (USAF), concluded that 'It is the American presence on the Continent that allays most of Germany's fears. It is American nuclear weapons in Germany … that provide her with guarantees against nuclear threats and blackmail … [and that are] the key for diluting both security and nonsecurity motivations for Germany to become a nuclear power'.[3]

## Turkey

Like Germany, Turkey has historically depended on US nuclear guarantees. Duygu Bazoglu Sezer, a prominent Turkish scholar, has pointed to her country's anxieties about the proliferation of weapons of mass destruction (WMD) in nearby nations. She has also noted Ankara's 'concern that Russia could use its nuclear arsenal to cajole and intimidate Turkey into retreating from the foreign policy objective of establishing close political, economic, and cultural relations with the newly independent states in the southern Caucasus and Central Asia'.[4] Some Russians have interpreted these Turkish aspirations as a quest for a sphere of political and economic influence at Moscow's expense in the Caucasus and Central Asia. According to this Russian view, Turkey, other NATO Allies and the Alliance as a whole rely on US nuclear protection for their economic and political expansion.

According to Sezer, Turkey's 'commitment to non-nuclear weapons status is coupled with several strong qualifiers'. The caveats associated with NATO and US nuclear commitments are perhaps the most significant:

> *the strategic balance between the United States and NATO*
> *and the Russian Federation must not be allowed to erode, by*
> *the former's unilateral moves to the disadvantage of NATO,*
> *until Russia gives sustained evidence that it has devalued the*
> *role of nuclear weapons in its overall foreign policy, includ-*
> *ing its policy toward the near abroad and their neighbors*
> *rather than merely in its Western policy ... In other words,*
> *the extended deterrence of the United States must remain*
> *convincing and credible to Turks as well as to* de facto *and*
> de jure *nuclear weapons states and potential proliferators.*[5]

Turkey's major political movements and its military establishment are committed to the nation remaining a non-nuclear-weapon state party to the Non-Proliferation Treaty (NPT), if NATO and US nuclear guarantees remain credible. According to Mustafa Kibaroglu, although a 'few Turkish politicians' – Islamic fundamentalists and extreme nationalists without decision-making influence – 'have made irresponsible and reckless statements' about a potential national nuclear capability, most of the allegations concerning a Turkey–Pakistan nuclear connection have emanated from sources in Greece and India, 'both of which are adversaries of one of the parties accused of being in illicit collaboration'.[6]

## Deterring Proliferation outside NATO

Since the end of the Cold War, officials of NATO governments have become more inclined to refer to non-Russian reasons for the US nuclear presence in Europe. Borrowing a term used at times in French discussions of nuclear issues, some have described NATO's posture as '*tous azimuts*' (all points of the compass). With the Russian rationale no longer explicit, adversaries that might need to be deterred with nuclear weapons could at some point include WMD-armed countries to the south and south-east of NATO Europe. Volker Rühe, then the German Minister of Defence, told the press after the October 1992 meeting of the NPG that 'There are no more nuclear weapons aimed at any concrete threat'. He added that 'These weapons insure us politically against risks that we cannot calculate, risks which might arise from the proliferation of weapons of mass destruction'.[7]

Rühe's statement implies that NATO now relies on what some have called an 'adaptive planning' approach – an *ad hoc* targeting capability. This could give the Alliance the flexibility to deal with threats that WMD proliferants may pose in the future. As Gregory Schulte, then NATO's Director for Nuclear Planning, noted in 1995, 'the Alliance could find itself faced with an Article 5 situation, possibly with little warning ... through a hostile country on NATO's periphery threatening or actually making use of WMD against Allied territory, population or forces'.[8]

The US nuclear presence in Europe forms part of NATO's military posture that may deter the acquisition or use of WMD. As Schulte puts it, the leaders of a

> *rogue government ... must be made to understand that the possession of weapons of mass destruction would not provide any political or military advantage but, rather, would cause them to incur enormous risks. Mounting such a deterrent requires the Alliance to have a balanced mix of active defence, passive defence and response capabilities, supported by good intelligence and effective command and control ... NATO's nuclear posture plays an essential role in making the risks of any aggression incalculable and unacceptable.*[9]

Deterring the acquisition of WMD may be difficult because procurement programmes are likely to be driven more by local and immediate ambitions and insecurities than by assessments of US and NATO capabilities and options. The Indian and Pakistani nuclear tests in May 1998, for example, evidently had an array of causes distant from concerns regarding the Atlantic Alliance. Domestic political and bureaucratic factors were critical. The Indian government emphasised its determination to respond to China's expansion and modernisation of its nuclear arsenal, as well as to Beijing's support for Pakistan's missile and nuclear programmes. New Delhi's interest in influencing Pakistani decision-making, plus its desire to enhance its prestige and strengthen its claim to permanent membership of the UN Security Council, may also have contributed to the decision to test.

*India and Pakistan have weakened non-proliferation norms*

Non-proliferation norms could be weakened by the general perception that India and Pakistan have suffered few consequences for breaking them. States already inclined to seek nuclear arms could exploit Indian and Pakistani behaviour to justify their choices. This would in turn exacerbate the insecurities of others, thereby increasing the likelihood of further nuclear proliferation. Proliferants could include Iran, Iraq and Libya, states which could pose threats to US interests. If would-be proliferants found nuclear weapons beyond their grasp, they might see greater incentives to pursue chemical or biological arms.

US nuclear weapons in Europe could send political signals (including a message of Alliance unity and determination) that might be helpful in crisis management *vis-à-vis* proliferants. In June 1996, NATO's Defence Planning Committee and NPG reported that:

> *Particular attention was given to enhancements to the Alliance's ability to move its forces within and between theatres and to sustain them once they are deployed. Such capabilities are essential both for the Alliance's collective defence and for new missions which require the capability for flexible deployments for defence, peacekeeping and crisis management and the capability to counter the risks of the proliferation of weapons of mass destruction and their means of delivery.*[10]

Dual-capable aircraft might be able to transmit more politically visible signals of Alliance solidarity, resolve and determination than US or British nuclear-armed submarines, or US nuclear systems based in North America.

In April 1996, the controversy over the apparent construction of an underground chemical-weapons plant at Tarhunah in Libya prompted then US Secretary of Defense William Perry to draw a distinction between military action to stop WMD production, and action in response to the use of WMD against the US. If diplomatic measures failed to persuade the Libyans to desist, the US might consider military action. According to Perry: 'That would not need to be, and I would never recommend, nuclear weapons for that particular application. So, any implication that we would use nuclear weapons for that purpose is just wrong'. He added that 'if some nation were to ... attack the United States with chemical weapons, then they would have to fear the consequences of a response from any weapon in our inventory ... In every situation that I have seen so far, nuclear weapons would not be required for response. That is, we could make a devastating response without the use of nuclear weapons, but we would not forswear that possibility'.[11]

In 1995, the US reaffirmed the negative security assurances (NSAs) given to non-nuclear-weapon states party to the NPT. Would these NSAs be an obstacle to retaliating with nuclear forces in response to an adversary's use of chemical or biological weapons? In December 1997, Robert Bell, the senior director for defence policy at the US National Security Council (NSC), stated that the presidential directive the previous month on nuclear-weapons policy reflected 'much greater sensitivity to the threats' posed by chemical and biological arms. According to Bell, 'if any nation uses weapons of mass destruction against the United States, it may "forfeit" its protection from US nuclear attack under the 1995 pledge'.[12] In practice, the strong preference of the US and the other Allies would be to avoid using nuclear weapons and to rely on conventional forces. However, as the statements by Perry and Bell suggest, Washington and its NATO Allies are reluctant to give up whatever deterrent value ambiguity may provide. Ashton Carter, then US Assistant Secretary of Defense for International Security Policy, and David Omand, at the time Deputy Under-Secretary (Policy) at the British Ministry of Defence, have argued that two principles must guide the Alliance's response to WMD proliferation. According to these officials, who served as co-chairmen of NATO's Senior Defence Group on Proliferation, NATO's response should 'complement nuclear deterrence with a mix of defensive and responsive conventional capabilities'. It should also 'balance a mix of capabilities including nuclear forces and conventional response capabilities to devalue a proliferant's NBC [nuclear, biological and chemical] weapons by denying the military advantages they would confer and through the prospect of an overwhelming response to their use'.[13]

Some commentators have argued that operational use of nuclear weapons (for instance, against a WMD production site or a concentration of WMD-armed delivery vehicles) might be small and still militarily effective. Some speculate that a nuclear weapon might be particularly well-suited to neutralising certain targets. The pathogens generated at a facility producing biological weapons might be spread by a conventional attack, whereas a nuclear weapon could provide the heat necessary to destroy them. However, the physical effects of nuclear weapons might be less controllable than predicted, and could have far-reaching political consequences. For Richard Dittbenner, it is:

> *an unproven assumption that a penetrating nuclear weapon fired into uncertain geological strata would not have ... unintended consequences ... Accidental atomic fallout drifting over our Mediterranean and Middle Eastern allies from a US nuclear explosion at Tarhunah could seriously erode or destroy the unstable political support we now have for our military presence in the region.*[14]

The political reactions in Western societies to either nuclear-signalling manoeuvres or the operational use of nuclear weapons might depend on the circumstances of the crisis. A deliberately publicised movement of US and Allied nuclear-capable aircraft, for example, might cause public anxiety. The possibility that nuclear weapons might actually be used could erode the legitimacy of the US nuclear posture in Europe among large sectors of the public in NATO countries, including the US. However, some have speculated that, if NATO forces were attacked with chemical or biological weapons in an intervention overseas, sustaining hundreds or thousands of fatalities, the public acceptability of nuclear retaliation might increase. Some have argued that such losses could even lead to an outcry demanding severe retaliation, including nuclear strikes, perhaps against isolated military targets.

Retaliatory nuclear operations would be distinct from conventional military actions undertaken at the outset of a war, or pre-emptive conventional destruction of WMD facilities. According to Michael Rühle:

> *NATO, given its democratic, multinational, and defensive nature, is incapable of any deliberately planned offensive action ... it is simply inconceivable that NATO Allies would find the political will to launch a preventive military strike*

*even against the facilities of a state which persisted in its development of WMD in the light of international opposition.*[15]

Some observers judge that the willingness of Allies to take collective action could increase if doing so was seen as necessary to prevent nuclear proliferation.

European–American differences over how to deal with such challenges – and what role to assign to US nuclear forces – could easily arise during a crisis. Disagreements among the NATO Allies over how to deal with proliferants in peacetime could also undermine WMD proliferation as a rationale for maintaining US nuclear weapons in Europe. The differences between the US and its West European Allies regarding relations with Iran, Libya and other 'rogue' states have long been apparent. West Europeans have in several cases rejected US attempts to impose diplomatic and economic isolation on these states. The long-term future of the UN Special Commission (UNSCOM) is also unclear, given the interest in trade with Baghdad shown by Russia, France and others.

*US–European differences over the role of US nuclear forces*

The Russian and WMD-proliferation rationales for maintaining the US nuclear presence in Europe could become increasingly incompatible if Russia and the US (and/or Russia and NATO) deepen their cooperation in non-proliferation activities. If democratisation and reform continued in Russia, and if the country became a NATO partner in efforts to counter proliferation, the Russian rationale for the US nuclear presence could atrophy. At the same time, the WMD-proliferation rationale might benefit from a tacit Russian endorsement.

On the other hand, if Russia became a major contributor to WMD-proliferant threats to NATO Europe, the Russian and WMD-proliferation rationales might become mutually reinforcing. Some Russians have raised the possibility of promoting nuclear proliferation in selected cases. Surikov has suggested that Russia could 'resort to selling its nuclear and missile military technologies to such countries as Iran, Iraq and Algeria'.[16] Russian officials have, however, generally asserted that their country has no interest in promoting the emergence of a nuclear-armed Iran, and that Russian nuclear assistance to Tehran has been limited to civilian reactors for electricity-generation. Despite Russia's long-term security interests, short-term economic imperatives could lead some Russians to pursue technology transfers beyond those officially acknowledged. (In July 1998 and January 1999, the US imposed trade sanctions on Russian organisations suspected of violating export controls regarding transfers of weapons technology to Iran and other states.) In any case, Iran's civilian nuclear-power programmes foster the development of a nuclear infrastructure and increase Tehran's nuclear expertise.

The South Asian nuclear tests in 1998 gave Russia an opportunity to reinvigorate its links with India in response to the Sino-Pakistani *entente*. Russia's assistance to India's submarine and missile programmes, civilian nuclear efforts and other military or dual-use activities might help to put Russia and India in a position to challenge either the West or China.[17] In some circumstances, Russia and India could threaten Allied interests and complicate or condition the types of missions which the US and some of its Allies might undertake outside the NATO area. 'Coalitions of the willing' comprising the US and some NATO Allies – even if not acting under Alliance auspices – would probably depend in part on US nuclear forces and commitments in Europe to protect support areas to the rear, and to deter certain kinds of attacks, especially those which might be conducted with WMD.

US nuclear forces and commitments in Europe have a dual function with regard to WMD proliferation. Credible US guarantees to Allies lessen the incentives to consider national nuclear-weapon programmes. At the same time, these forces provide the Alliance with options which may be useful, in conjunction with conventional response capabilities and other policy instruments, in dealing with WMD proliferants.

*chapter 3*

# West European Cooperation

The possibility that West European nuclear-weapon cooperation could affect US nuclear commitments to European security might seem to have been given a new lease of life by France's *dissuasion concertée* initiative in 1995. This, however, is almost certainly not the case. The substantial obstacles to effective cooperation on a wider European basis make it doubtful whether any substitute for US nuclear guarantees can be devised within the next ten to 15 years. Indeed, according to a June 1996 statement by President Jacques Chirac, France does not aim 'to substitute a French or Franco-British guarantee for the American deterrent. We want a reinforcement of the overall deterrent'.[1]

Nonetheless, genuine progress has been made in the Franco-British nuclear dialogue. A Joint Commission on Nuclear Policy and Doctrine was established in 1992–93. Little information has been published about its deliberations, but the two nations seem to have found a greater similarity in their thinking than was anticipated at the outset. The main public achievement has been a joint statement in October 1995. Chirac and John Major, at the time British Prime Minister, declared that 'We do not see situations arising in which the vital interests of either France or the United Kingdom could be threatened without the vital interests of the other also being threatened'. The two leaders added that:

*We have decided to pursue and deepen nuclear cooperation between our two countries. Our aim is mutually to strengthen deterrence, while retaining the independence of our nuclear forces. The deepening of cooperation between the two European members of the North Atlantic Alliance who are nuclear powers will therefore strengthen the European contribution to overall deterrence.[2]*

## Dissuasion Concertée

In January and August–September 1995, senior French officials advanced what seemed to be new proposals for consultations with European partners about France's nuclear deterrent. Then Prime Minister Alain Juppé called for the work of the Joint Commission to be carried forward. He also called for Germany – 'our closest ally' – to be included in a dialogue on nuclear-weapon matters within the European Union (EU). Juppé explained that Paris was not proposing 'extended deterrence' (*dissuasion élargie*) – that is, France protecting Germany – because this could 'lend itself to a suspicion of paternalism' in German perceptions.[3] Other French officials explained that this was also not a proposal for 'shared deterrence' (*dissuasion partagée*), partly because the EU was far from establishing a common executive for a true political union. Juppé and other French officials suggested that it would be better to speak of *dissuasion concertée*. The phrase 'deterrence supported by continuing consultations and substantive consensus' conveys what the French evidently have in mind.

In January 1997, the publicity surrounding the Franco-German 'common concept for security and defence', approved in December 1996 by Chirac and then German Chancellor Helmut Kohl, drew new attention to the initiative. According to the concept:

*The supreme guarantee of the security of the Allies is provided by the strategic nuclear forces of the Alliance, particularly those of the United States; the independent nuclear forces of the United Kingdom and France, which have a deterrent role of their own, contribute to the overall deterrence and security of the Allies. Our countries are ready to engage in a dialogue concerning the function of nuclear deterrence in the context of European defence policy.[4]*

The controversy provoked by this paragraph obliged senior French authorities to point out how closely it paralleled the Alliance's 1974 Ottawa Declaration and 1991 Strategic Concept, and to minimise the extent to which it involved new thinking. Some French sources have suggested that *dissuasion concertée* might involve a process extending over a generation. Since the change of government in June 1997, in which Lionel Jospin replaced Juppé as Prime Minister, the French have tended to refer to 'the nuclear dimension of European construction' or similar formulae, instead of *dissuasion concertée*. In September 1997, both Chirac and Jospin confirmed France's continuing interest in an intra-West European dialogue on nuclear-weapon matters.[5] Such statements have, however, become increasingly rare. The obstacles to pursuing the concept rapidly have become undeniable in view of the reactions to it, both in Europe and in France itself.

### Obstacles within Europe

Within Europe, there are several stumbling-blocks to *dissuasion concertée*. The British have consistently declared that France should follow the same approach to nuclear consultations in NATO as do the UK and the US. As then Secretary of State for Defence Malcolm Rifkind put it in 1992: 'It is not in our interests to encourage any tendency towards thinking that there could be a major conflict in Europe in which

*European scepticism about* **dissuasion concertée**

the question of nuclear use arose which did not involve the vital interests of all the allies including the US'.[6] In 1995, as Foreign Secretary, Rifkind made the same point in responding to the *dissuasion concertée* proposal: 'if they [the French] wish to see their nuclear deterrent not simply for the national defence of France but also part of the wider defence of Europe, the ultimate conclusion would be consistent with the British and American approach to nuclear weapons for the last fifty years'.[7]

Germany's priority remains protecting NATO's nuclear-consultation process and US nuclear commitments. The Germans have long made clear that the US nuclear guarantee is valued far more highly than anything the French could offer. Then Defence Minister Volker Rühe stated in September 1995 that 'for us nothing can replace NATO's nuclear umbrella'. Even Germans who supported the French proposal took care to specify that the French deterrent should complement US nuclear commitments.[8] German media commentary was generally sceptical about the French proposal's credibility and utility.[9] The proposal would, it was pointed out, extend France's definition of 'vital interests' to include Germany and other non-nuclear EU members of NATO. It would also encompass neutral EU states, such as Ireland and Sweden, which have not favoured endorsements of the value of nuclear deterrence. Some Germans expressed concern that the proposal could prompt a disengagement of US nuclear commitments. Germany – governed by a Social Democratic Party (SPD)–Green coalition since October 1998 – is likely to be cautious about any dialogue with France on nuclear deterrence.

NATO's European nations generally oppose any European-only framework that might undermine NATO and US nuclear commitments. A French proposal in January 1996 for nuclear discussions in the North Atlantic Council (NAC) was received warily because of concern that it might weaken the NPG and its associated bodies. The US and the other NPG participants have shown no interest in modifying or dismantling existing nuclear-consultation structures to accommodate the French. Some well-placed French observers recognise that it would be contrary to French and to NATO European security interests to do so if it undermined US nuclear commitments to Europe.

## Obstacles within France

French membership in NATO's NPG would be the most practical solution to the dilemma of retaining US nuclear commitments, while making France's commitment to its allies explicit. This course has been recommended by British and German observers, and has been pursued by the UK since 1967. Numerous French politicians and commentators have, however, argued since the late 1960s that NPG participation would represent subordination to the US and the end of an autonomous national nuclear strategy. Many French observers argue that NPG participation would be 'too strong a symbol' of NATO integration in the country's domestic politics. Non-participation is seen as a proof of France's sovereignty and strategic independence. Some French observers even believe that the US dominates the NPG to the resentment of European participants, who are obliged to be passive recipients of American policy guidance; that NPG membership would attenuate French sovereignty over nuclear decisions, with the Supreme Allied Commander Europe (SACEUR) somehow taking control of French nuclear forces; that the US has reduced the UK to such a state of dependence that London no longer controls its own nuclear forces; and that NATO's strategy of 'flexible response' called for extensive battlefield use of nuclear weapons in support of conventional operations, in contrast to France's more 'political' war-termination approach.

Nonetheless, some French observers acknowledge that participating in the NPG would offer advantages. It would improve the Allies' ability to act coherently and effectively in a nuclear-related crisis; make France's commitment to collective defence less ambiguous; strengthen the European 'pillar' within NATO; enhance France's credibility as a 'team player' in the Alliance; and help to 'lock in' US security commitments, including nuclear guarantees, to NATO Europe. It remains unclear, however, whether the long-entrenched French views about the NPG can be overcome.

France's reluctance to place its deterrent posture within an Alliance framework may be an even greater obstacle to pursuing *dissuasion concertée*. The French have been accustomed to making nuclear decisions on a national basis. Almost all of Chirac's important decisions regarding nuclear forces have been taken without consultation with Allies. The sole exception was the February 1996 decision to eliminate the *Hadès* missiles, which was taken after consulting Kohl – for which Chirac was criticised in some political circles.

Any impression that Paris was accepting advice from its Allies on its nuclear posture could create domestic political difficulties. French officials might not welcome scrutiny by Allied governments of the country's doctrine and force characteristics. For some years at least, the French are likely to be uncomfortable with the principle of assigning forces for NATO planning, even though national planning options could also be pursued, as in the US and British cases. While France assigned aircraft to NATO command organisations for the *Deny Flight* operation in Bosnia, cooperation regarding nuclear-capable aircraft could be much more sensitive. Some Gaullists have deplored *dissuasion concertée* as dangerous since it implies taking nuclear risks on behalf of France's neighbours, and listening to foreign views that might constrain the country's decision-making autonomy in nuclear matters. Influential observers closely associated with the late President François Mitterrand and prominent Socialists have argued that nuclear deterrence may be an unsuitable foundation on which to build a European defence identity.[10]

## Implications for US Forces and Commitments

French proponents of *dissuasion concertée* believe that it could increase the legitimacy and political acceptance of French nuclear forces in the EU and the Western European Union (WEU) as a contribution to the security of France's partners and an element of the EU's Common Foreign and Security Policy (CFSP). The fundamental assumption behind at least some articulations of *dissuasion concertée* is that US nuclear guarantees may be unreliable, and that Western Europe must therefore lessen its dependence on the US. Some French observers have argued that an arsenal of hundreds of survivable SLBM warheads, based on British and French ballistic-missile submarines (SSBNs), would be sufficient to dissuade Russia from aggression or coercion against Western Europe.

However, the more widely endorsed view in Europe has been that only nuclear capabilities comparable in size to Russia's (that is, those of the US) can reliably balance Moscow's forces and protect NATO Europe. In 1988, Christoph Bertram, then foreign-affairs editor of *Die Zeit* and a former IISS Director, wrote that, from a German perspective, British and French nuclear forces 'do not provide deterrence beyond the narrowest definition of British and French national security'.[11] Reactions in Germany and elsewhere in NATO Europe to France's 1995 initiatives confirm that this assessment has not changed. If a group of European nations under EU, WEU or other auspices succeeded in building a collective 'Eurodeterrent', some Americans might conclude that US commitments and forces in Europe were no longer necessary.

France has a great deal of expertise and capability to offer, in a context in which NATO will have a less diversified and less redundant nuclear arsenal than in the past. France will remain the only NATO country with nuclear-armed air-launched missiles in Europe. If French worries about the NPG can be overcome, it may be possible for the UK, France and the US to cooperate more closely and to cultivate a more intensive dialogue with the non-nuclear NATO Allies about potential future nuclear challenges, within and beyond Europe. The 'concertation' in *dissuasion concertée* would, in other words, be NATO-wide, rather than (as the French have proposed) limited to Europeans, excluding the US and implying that US nuclear commitments are unreliable. As Karl-Heinz Kamp has observed, 'From a German viewpoint any European nuclear entity can only be one part of a European–transatlantic security structure'.[12]

## chapter 4

# 'Delegitimisation' and Arms Control

## Nuclear-Abolitionist Advocacy

Mass public feeling and protest movements against nuclear weapons and deterrence policies in Western societies could have direct implications for the future of US nuclear forces and commitments in Europe. However, since the anti-nuclear protest movements of the late 1970s and early 1980s, no politically potent demands for the withdrawal of US nuclear weapons have emerged. Some non-governmental organisations (NGOs) on both sides of the Atlantic have advocated removing these weapons as a step towards achieving a world without nuclear arms. These groups have influenced the policy preferences of individual officials in NATO governments, but historically most Alliance administrations have found the security arguments for maintaining US nuclear forces and commitments in Europe persuasive.

Since the end of the Cold War, several advocacy groups have championed the elimination of nuclear weapons as a practical, short- or medium-term (as opposed to ultimate) goal. These groups have argued for intermediate steps that could directly affect US nuclear forces and commitments in Europe. In August 1996, the Canberra Commission on the Elimination of Nuclear Weapons called for 'immediate and determined efforts ... to rid the world of nuclear weapons'. The Commission suggested that the nuclear powers should make reciprocal no-first-use pledges and 'remove all non-strategic nuclear weapons from deployed sites to a limited number of secure storage facilities on their territory'.[1] In December 1996, a group of mainly Russian and US retired military officers argued that less specific measures, including further de-alerting of strategic nuclear forces and substantial cutbacks in US and Russian forces, could help to create 'a nuclear-weapons-free world'.[2] The Canberra Commission and other advocacy organisations have been encouraged by a July 1996 advisory opinion by the International Court of Justice (ICJ). The opinion held that there is 'an obligation to pursue in good faith and bring to a conclusion negotiations leading to nuclear disarmament in all its aspects under strict and effective international control'.[3]

Attempts to delegitimise nuclear weapons and promote their abolition in the near future have achieved little resonance and credibility with NATO governments. The consensus in official circles appears to be that, while nuclear disarmament remains an ultimate goal in conjunction with general disarmament, in the foreseeable future nuclear deterrence will remain valuable for Western security.[4] In December 1996, the US Executive issued a press statement rejecting recommendations advanced by some abolitionist groups. According to the statement, 'we do not believe that removing nuclear weapons from alert status and placing the warheads in controlled storage or further restricting US nuclear declaratory policy is in our security interests'.[5]

## The ICJ Opinion

In its 1996 advisory, the ICJ held, in a seven-to-seven opinion decided by the presiding judge's vote, that:

> *the threat or use of nuclear weapons would generally be contrary to the rules of international law applicable in armed conflict, and in particular the principles and rules of humanitarian law. However, in view of the current state of international law, and of the elements of fact at its disposal, the Court cannot conclude definitively whether the threat or use of nuclear weapons would be lawful or unlawful in an extreme circumstance of self-defence, in which the very survival of a State would be at stake.[6]*

The Court held unanimously that 'A threat or use of force by means of nuclear weapons that is contrary to Article 2, paragraph 4, of the United Nations Charter and that fails to meet all the requirements of Article 51, is unlawful'.[7] In other words, the threat or use of nuclear weapons – or any other weapon, for that matter – for aggression or coercion 'against the territorial integrity or political independence of any state' (prohibited by Article 2, paragraph 4) would be unlawful, as would be the use of nuclear weapons for purposes other than 'the inherent right of individual or collective self-defence' (authorised by Article 51).

Some Western experts have seen this part of the Court's opinion as vindicating official policies, given NATO's orientation towards war-prevention, deterrence, maintaining international peace and security, and (if necessary) self-defence to protect vital interests.[8] The briefs to the ICJ submitted by four of the five NPT-recognised nuclear-weapon states – France, Russia, the UK and the US – made clear that they consider their policies to be legal. (China submitted no brief, but evidently has no doubts about the legality of its policies.) No nuclear-weapon power has revealed any plans to change its policies as a result of the ICJ's advisory, which has no legally binding force.

## The Impact of Abolitionist Advocacy

To the extent that Western governments have reacted to the arguments of advocacy groups, their views have been similar to those expressed by Walter Slocombe in February 1997. Slocombe stated that 'Abolition, if understood as a near-term policy, rather than, as President Clinton has stated, an ultimate goal, is not a wise and surely not a feasible focus of policy'.[9] He directly challenged arguments advanced by abolitionist groups, for instance the notion that 'The possession of nuclear weapons by any state is a constant stimulus to other states to acquire them'.[10] As Slocombe pointed out:

> *proliferant states acquire nuclear weapons not because we have them but for reasons of their own – to counter regional adversaries, to further regional ambitions, and to enhance their status among their neighbors ... The incentives to proliferate would hardly be reduced if a rogue state would,*

> *through a successful nuclear weapons program, acquire a*
> *nuclear monopoly, not a token capability facing far stronger*
> *forces possessed by the US and other world powers ... our*
> *nuclear capabilities are more likely to give pause to potential*
> *rogue proliferants than encourage them.*

Furthermore, US extended deterrence 'has removed incentives for key allies, in a still dangerous world, to develop and deploy their own nuclear forces, as many are technically capable of doing'.[11]

Abolitionist groups are unlikely to attract much public attention or change government policies unless there is a grave accident or crisis involving nuclear weapons, nuclear arms are actually used in a conflict, or Russia resorts to reckless rhetoric. Historically, the fear of a war in which nuclear weapons might be used and rhetoric implying rashness in nuclear-weapon policy from Washington or Moscow have prompted large protest demonstrations, as in 1958–62 and 1979–83. Even in times of intense public anxiety, however, Western governments have resisted the pressure of demonstrations and opinion polls. As Kohl observed in 1992:

> *Political leadership also means not following the mood of the*
> *moment in existential issues. If Konrad Adenauer had fol-*
> *lowed public opinion polls our country would never have*
> *become a member of the North Atlantic Alliance ... If I had*
> *followed public opinion polls in 1982/83, then the NATO*
> *dual track decision would never have been implemented. As*
> *Mikhail Gorbachev himself told me, however, it was precisely*
> *the unity and steadfastness of the Alliance in the early 1980s*
> *that contributed to the 'new thinking' of the Soviet leadership*
> *and in the final analysis also to German unification.*[12]

Some observers have speculated that delegitimisation could result from the fading away of any plausible threat that might require nuclear deterrence. Such speculation may prove well-founded, but the inertia of public attitudes suggests that specific events are more likely to provoke delegitimisation. Historically, attitudes towards nuclear deterrence in the US and other Western societies have amounted to resigned ambivalence – a distaste for nuclear weapons and a reluctance to contemplate their operational use, but a judgment that they are probably necessary for deterrence and war-prevention. This ambivalence seems to be stable unless aroused by fear.[13]

Various types of events could erode the legitimacy of the US nuclear presence in Europe. The possibility of an accident involving US nuclear forces is generally judged to be remote, but it is not non-existent. Even if an accident entailed little or no release of radioactivity, there might, depending on the circumstances, be a public uproar regarding a possible 'military Chernobyl'. If the accident involved contamination and loss of life, it

*the inertia of public opinion protects the status quo*

could threaten the sustainability of the US nuclear presence in Europe. However, NATO has for many years invested in improving the safety and security of weapons, storage sites and associated equipment and procedures.

Conventional military operations in Europe could inadvertently threaten the security of US nuclear weapons. The accidental bombing of a nuclear-storage site could be presented as proof of the risks of basing such weapons in Europe – even if no weapons were damaged, no radioactive materials were released, and US custody over the weapons was never jeopardised. An accident involving US, British, French or Russian nuclear arms or naval nuclear-propulsion systems – or even a significant nuclear-reactor accident in Europe or elsewhere – could raise questions about the advisability of maintaining US nuclear weapons in Europe.

In 1986, Merrill Walters, at the time NATO's Director for Nuclear Planning, wrote that 'An attack [by terrorists] on our nuclear forces could indeed have a very high public and political impact, even if unsuccessful'.[14] The Alliance established a Senior Level Weapons Protection Group (SLWPG) in 1982 to improve the security of nuclear-storage sites. All US nuclear weapons in Europe contain modern safety, security and use-control features, and by late 1998 the programme to store all weapons in underground vaults was almost complete. As a result, the functions of the SLWPG were subsumed into the NPG's High Level Group in December 1998.

There has been speculation about the risk that nuclear weapons might be used in a regional conflict, perhaps in South Asia or the Middle East/Persian Gulf. South Asia has attracted greater attention since the Indian and Pakistani nuclear tests in 1998, with concern about the possible use of nuclear weapons, either deliberately or through miscalculation. Developments in South Asia may increase the risks of proliferation in East Asia and the Middle East/ Persian Gulf, with states inclined to pursue nuclear arms taking the opportunity to do so presented by a perceived lapse in the non-proliferation regime.

If nuclear weapons were used in a conflict unconnected with NATO or US military forces, the reactions in Western societies would probably include horror and revulsion. There could also be demands for security policies free from dependence on nuclear weapons – including US nuclear arms in Europe. Relying on nuclear weapons for deterrence, war-prevention and political stabilisation, to say nothing of threatening their use for crisis-management in collective-defence contingencies, might seem to many to have become excessively risky.

Other sectors of Western societies might nonetheless demand that US nuclear forces and commitments in Europe be maintained. Whether deliberately or through miscalculation, the detonation of nuclear weapons in a conflict distant from Europe might increase the reluctance of the Allies to give up their nuclear-deterrence arrangements. Fearful and wary governments might be inclined to maintain or even reinforce their defence postures, partly because abandoning capabilities and diminishing their political and military options might be interpreted as a sign of weakness.

A crisis in which NATO faced the prospect of actually using US nuclear weapons could lead to acrimonious public debates in parliaments and other fora of opinion in Alliance nations. The overriding imperative would probably be to find conventional ways to deal with the challenge which provoked the crisis, and to avoid a decision on using nuclear weapons. In the aftermath of the crisis, US nuclear weapons in Europe might be seen as a source of trouble and risk, rather than as one of the means of ensuring NATO's security.

If US nuclear-deterrence commitments were ever actually tested by aggression against NATO that could not be effectively countered by conventional means, it would be important that such behaviour receive a forceful, prompt and collective NATO response. If not, the credibility of US extended deterrence would at the least be questioned. Even 'successful' operational use of nuclear weapons by

NATO – that is, a decisive role in ending a war – could have negative effects on the legitimacy of the nuclear posture, owing in part to the implications of breaking the 'nuclear taboo'. If a state such as Iraq used nuclear weapons against Israel or Saudi Arabia and thereby gained political leverage, some in NATO countries could see a rationale for continued reliance on nuclear-deterrence capabilities and for greater NATO involvement in 'out-of-area' security problems. It must be acknowledged, however, that 'NATO is still a long way from defining itself as a coalition of those willing to export stability to regional theatres outside of Europe'.[15] Much would depend on whether the people of Allied states solidly supported the operation, or were uneasy about what might be portrayed as a US-driven venture with a NATO label. For many, the reaction might be the same, whatever the initial level of Alliance cohesion and whatever the circumstances – revulsion and demands for the abolition of all nuclear weapons, starting perhaps with the US arms based in Europe.

## Arms Control

At least four types of arms-control negotiations or arrangements might affect US nuclear weapons in Europe, either explicitly or indirectly. These are: a treaty regime limiting or eliminating the remaining weapons; the CTBT; nuclear-weapons-free zones in Europe or adjacent regions; and pressures for nuclear disarmament related to non-proliferation.

### A Treaty Regime

Various organisations and analysts have suggested negotiations to limit or, more typically, eliminate the remaining US nuclear weapons in Europe. However, most attention has focused on the arms-control ideas advanced by governments, particularly Russia and the US. In September 1991, President George Bush proposed a number of reciprocal unilateral adjustments in the US and Soviet nuclear-weapon postures. These were accepted by Soviet President Mikhail Gorbachev, who then proposed that 'on a reciprocal basis, we could remove from active units of front tactical aviation all nuclear ammunition bombs and aircraft missiles and destroy them'.[16] Gorbachev's suggestion was consistent with long-standing Soviet efforts to see the US nuclear presence in Europe removed entirely, and the US did not accept it. The Russians have, however, intermittently continued to express interest in such concepts. In September 1994, Pavel Grachev, then Minister of Defence, advocated destroying all 'tactical nuclear weapons, including those delivered by aircraft'.[17]

No US authorities have proposed negotiations to eliminate these weapons, but they have been mentioned as a possible topic for discussion. In September 1994, Deputy Secretary of Defense Deutch stated that 'we are extremely eager to work with the Russians on reducing the number of weapons that they have as rapidly as possible, down to the levels that we've already reduced to, especially in the area of non-strategic nuclear forces'.[18] In March 1997, Clinton and Yeltsin 'agreed that in the context of START III negotiations their experts will explore, as separate issues, possible measures relating to nuclear long-range sea-launched cruise missiles and tactical nuclear systems, to include appropriate confidence-building and trans-parency measures'.[19]

It is unclear whether discussions on 'tactical' or 'non-strategic' nuclear forces will be productive. The US has already withdrawn most of the weapons in question and has dismantled a large number of them.[20] In contrast, the Russians are believed to have well over 10,000 of these weapons, and to have made much less headway in dismantling them.[21] In February 1997, Slocombe testified that 'While Russia pledged in 1991 to make significant cuts in its non-strategic nuclear forces [NSNF] and has reduced its operational NSNF substantially, it has made far less progress thus far than the US, and the Russian non-strategic arsenal (deployed and stockpiled) is probably about ten times as large as ours'.[22] In March 1998, US Assistant Secretary of Defense Edward Warner repeated this estimate, adding that 'Russian officials recently stated that the 1991–1992 NSNF pledges would be fully implemented by the year 2000, which would reduce the Russian advantage to about three or four to one'.[23] In February 1998, Alain Richard, the French Minister of Defence, stated that Russia's 'stockpile of so-called tactical [nuclear] weapons … is estimated to be between 10,000 and 30,000 warheads, and we have only fragmentary information on their control'.[24]

Russia's apparent numerical superiority in non-strategic forces means that it has little obvious incentive to eliminate them, or to reduce their numbers to US levels. The Alliance has repeatedly noted that:

> *At a time when NATO has vastly reduced its nuclear forces, Russia still retains a large number of tactical nuclear weapons of all types. We call upon Russia to bring to completion the reductions in these forces announced in 1991 and 1992, and to further review its tactical nuclear weapons stockpile with a view towards making additional significant reductions.*[25]

Russia's willingness to accept reductions in its non-strategic forces will almost certainly be limited given its conventional weakness and the threats it perceives on its periphery. The Russians might propose limits on non-strategic forces applying only to Europe, in view of their concerns about China and other powers in Asia. These limits might be much more readily circumvented by Russia than by the US and its Allies in NATO. Even if honoured in ordinary circumstances, they might be rapidly discarded in a crisis.

For Europeans, there is little practical difference between 'tactical' and 'strategic' Russian nuclear weapons. For some, given Russia's enormous number of weapons, a radical reduction in – or elimination of – its non-strategic nuclear arms is worth the price of removing US weapons from Europe. The Russians might use such proposals to try to drive a wedge between the Allies by promising to make large reductions in their non-strategic arms only if the US repatriated its weapons. Whatever the hopes in the Alliance, such an initiative is unlikely to result in effective arms control that would alleviate NATO's concerns about Russia's non-strategic forces.

*multiple problems in non-strategic arms control*

Indeed, multiple problems would arise in any effort to achieve meaningful arms control for non-strategic weapons in Europe. The verification challenges would be severe, since these weapons are much less readily observable than, for example, ICBMs. Initialisation or baseline numbers on the Russian side could not be easily established, at least in the eyes of cautious officials in Alliance governments. The problems of geographically defining 'Europe' and safeguarding against Russian covert redeployment could argue for global limitations. This would raise issues not only of territorial scope, but also of participants, for example China as well as the four nuclear powers in Europe.

It would be imperative to avoid eliminating US nuclear forces in Europe in a sort of 'unilateral denuclearisation', in which Russian non-strategic weapons would remain present, possibly in great numbers. To maintain the credibility of US extended deterrence and the benefits to Alliance cohesion of sharing roles and responsibilities, a significant level of US nuclear forces would have to be retained. Reconciling the requirements of extended deterrence with those of arms control may become one of the Alliance's future nuclear tasks.

For some politicians and analysts in NATO countries, US nuclear forces in Europe may increasingly appear more valuable as 'bargaining chips' to influence the safety, security and dismantling of Russian nuclear weapons and infrastructure, than as instruments to honour US extended-deterrence commitments. Some of the greatest nuclear uncertainties facing NATO concern the reliability of Russia's measures to protect its nuclear forces from theft, tampering, accidents and diversion. The feasibility of establishing arrangements for arms control and confidence-building is, however, unclear given Russia's interest in maintaining robust nuclear capabilities. The NATO–Russia PJC may provide a vehicle for dialogue that could encourage the Russians to be more transparent and to accept reductions in their non-strategic forces, despite the reported disappointments for NATO in the initial exchanges in this forum.

### The Comprehensive Test Ban Treaty and Nuclear-Weapons-Free Zones

Some observers argue that the CTBT could raise long-term risks since it would no longer be possible to test weapons to ensure reliability. This could undermine confidence in US nuclear weapons, potentially including those deployed in Europe.

US policy holds that a Stockpile Stewardship and Management Program will ensure 'a high level of confidence in the safety and reliability of nuclear weapons in the active stockpile' under a CTBT regime. The other US CTBT safeguards include the capability to resume testing, and procedures to withdraw from the CTBT under a 'supreme national interests' clause if 'a high level of confidence in the safety or reliability of a nuclear weapon type ... critical to our nuclear deterrent could no longer be certified'.[26] However, it remains to be seen whether and to what extent the stockpile-stewardship programmes currently envisaged will be effective. The feasibility of maintaining nuclear-weapon stockpiles in good order for decades without testing is by definition unproven.

Another arms-control challenge concerns proposals for nuclear-weapons-free zones in Europe. In April 1996, Yurii Baturin, Yeltsin's national-security adviser, suggested that such a zone be established in Central and Eastern Europe, including Belarus and Ukraine. Baturin hinted that 'Russia might drop its opposition to NATO's eastward expansion if his proposal were put into force'.[27] Also in 1996, Gennady Udovenko, then Ukraine's Foreign Minister, and other proponents of a nuclear-weapons-free zone in Central and Eastern Europe cited Norway as an example of a NATO nation that does not permit nuclear weapons on its soil.[28] Oslo's policy is, however, unilateral and open to revision in times of crisis or conflict.

Such a regime would oblige new NATO members in Central and Eastern Europe to remain free of nuclear weapons. This would rule out sharing roles and responsibilities with fellow allies, whatever the future circumstances. Establishing such a regime might complicate further NATO enlargement and might also undermine the legitimacy of the US nuclear presence in Europe. NATO governments and prospective Alliance members have criticised proposals for a nuclear-weapons-free zone in Central and Eastern Europe and are unlikely to find them attractive in the foreseeable future. In May 1998, Bulgaria, Croatia, the Czech Republic, Hungary, Poland, Romania, Slovakia and Slovenia stated jointly that establishing nuclear-weapons-free zones 'must not interfere with existing – or evolving – security arrangements to the detriment of regional and international security, or otherwise adversely affect the inalienable right to individual or collective self-defence guaranteed under the UN Charter'. Such a zone in Central and Eastern Europe would be 'incompatible with our sovereign resolve to contribute to, and benefit from, the new European security architecture ... including the North Atlantic Treaty Organization and the European Union'.[29]

In April 1996, the US signed protocols to the Treaty of Pelindaba, creating a nuclear-weapons-free zone in Africa. The treaty commits the nuclear-weapon-state signatories not to use or threaten to use nuclear weapons against signatories which are not nuclear-weapon states. Depending on how the US and its Allies interpret their obligations under treaties such as Pelindaba, they could undermine one of the rationales for maintaining US nuclear forces in Europe, at least with respect to deterring proliferants in Africa armed with 'only' chemical and/or biological weapons.

A variation on this theme is the concept, endorsed by Yeltsin in April 1996, that nuclear weapons should be based solely at sea or on the territory of their owners. In July 1996, as part of its decision to accept a nuclear-test moratorium in anticipation of the CTBT, China 'asked all countries with nuclear weapons deployed outside their borders to withdraw them'.[30] Such an arrangement would entail no penalties for China, but it would require the US to remove its nuclear forces from Europe.

## Pressures for Nuclear Disarmament

Some approaches to discouraging nuclear proliferation could become rationales for removing US nuclear weapons from Europe. Proponents of nuclear disarmament have argued that withdrawing these weapons would reduce incentives for other countries to seek nuclear arms.[31] At the opening of the NPT Review and Extension Conference in April 1995, Greenpeace and other NGOs argued that the US nuclear weapons in Europe, and the associated programmes of cooperation with non-nuclear Allies, were inconsistent with the NPT.[32]

In May 1995, while extending the NPT indefinitely, the Conference approved a document calling for the 'determined pursuit by the nuclear-weapon States of systematic and progressive efforts to reduce nuclear weapons globally, with the ultimate goal of eliminating those weapons'.[33] In June 1996, India repeated its long-standing arguments for a 'step-by-step process aimed at achieving complete elimination of all nuclear weapons within a time-bound framework'. New Delhi cited the refusal of nuclear-weapon states to accept a specific deadline for eliminating their nuclear arms as one of its justifications for not

*is the climate growing less hospitable to nuclear weapons?*

accepting what was then the draft CTBT.[34] In December 1998, a parliamentary committee in Ottawa recommended that 'Canada work consistently to reduce the political legitimacy and value of nuclear weapons in order to contribute to the goal of their progressive reduction and eventual elimination'.[35] These general pressures for nuclear disarmament as a way of promoting non-proliferation are not specific to US nuclear forces and commitments in Europe. They could nonetheless contribute to attitudes inhospitable to their maintenance.

## chapter 5

# Possible Changes in US Policy

Some concepts regarding the future of US nuclear forces and commitments in Europe may be characterised as technical adjustments. These include modernisation and improved command-and-control security. Although other ideas are sometimes described as merely technical adjustments, because the US would retain its nuclear commitments to the security of its Allies in NATO, they would in fact bring about more far-reaching change. Proposals for 'reconstitution' arrangements – deploying weapons in Europe only when a crisis required it – and concepts of US extended-deterrence commitments based solely on systems at sea and in the US would be a major departure from current practice, with potentially far-reaching implications. Modifying US strategic nuclear forces and missile-defence capabilities could also have implications for extended deterrence in Europe.

## Adjustments in the Existing Posture in Europe

In June 1996, NATO's Defence Planning Committee and the NPG announced that 'In the light of the changing security environment in Europe, NATO's nuclear forces have been substantially reduced, they are no longer targeted against anyone and the readiness of NATO's dual-capable aircraft has been recently adapted'.[1] Changes in readiness levels may be characterised as marginal. Some experts maintain that the numbers of US nuclear weapons have been reduced to such a low level that it is difficult to envisage further cutbacks, while others believe that more reductions are possible. Cutting the number of weapons and/or consolidating them at an even smaller number of storage sites could complicate efforts to achieve widespread participation in the sharing of nuclear roles and responsibilities. Moreover, given the investment already made in secure storage sites, it is doubtful whether such an approach would lead to significant savings unless air bases were closed entirely. Many of the costs involved in the dual-capable-aircraft posture would be undertaken anyway, so long as the US intends to maintain the conventional strike capabilities associated with these squadrons.

No proposal for modernising the US nuclear posture in Europe in the short term is likely. If such a proposal were made, it could place nuclear weapons at the centre of the Alliance's agenda and stimulate a debate that would be not only divisive and counter-productive, but also unnecessary since it appears that no modernisation will be needed for at least the next ten to 15 years. If and when modernisation is pursued, it may include a programme for stand-off (air-launched) missiles, which would offer advantages in attacking defended targets. According to published reports, an earth-penetrating version of the B-61 – the B-61-11, a modified nuclear bomb – has begun deployment in the US. Like all B-61s, the B-61-11 is a gravity bomb, not a warhead for a stand-off missile. The US has no plans to deploy the B-61-11 in Europe. Modernising the delivery mechanism, for example in the form of a stand-off missile, or the warhead itself is improbable unless substantially different political and strategic circumstances emerge to make a more operationally effective capability relevant.

*no modernisation is likely in the short term*

Some US and European observers have suggested relying on a 'reconstitution' approach to US nuclear forces in Europe. In essence, this would mean deploying US nuclear weapons in NATO Europe only if a crisis requiring their presence arose.[2] This approach would, however, pose political and strategic problems, even with periodic redeployment exercises. The argument that US nuclear weapons could always be brought back to Europe in an emergency is ill-founded. Many politicians and commentators would argue that any redeployment during a crisis would be perceived as 'escalatory', 'provoking' a WMD-armed adversary to take pre-emptive action.

Reconstitution would also fail to provide the important political 'reassurance' and the benefits of Allied participation offered by a continuing presence.

Many experts in NATO Europe judge that US guarantees would be less credible if backed only by sea-based and intercontinental strike systems. General Carlo Jean, the Director of Italy's Centre for Higher Defence Studies and a military adviser to the Italian President, has written that: 'A stable conflict prevention system cannot be without a minimal nuclear force in the European theatre. This function cannot be carried out by external nuclear forces nor by "second strike" nuclear forces, i.e. forces for deterring the enemy's nuclear forces'.[3] David Omand, then an official in the UK's Ministry of Defence, pointed out in June 1996 that 'all Allies agree on the importance of US weapons being stationed on the territory of some European Allies; and on their being available to be carried by Allied aircraft'.[4]

The arguments in support of relying on US nuclear forces outside Europe to provide extended deterrence often hinge on a 'target coverage' perspective. It is argued that the US need not maintain nuclear weapons and dual-capable aircraft in Europe because it could employ alternative means to strike targets in Russia or elsewhere. These could include submarine-launched or intercontinental ballistic missiles, *Tomahawk* land-attack missiles with nuclear warheads (TLAM-Ns), B-2 bombers armed with gravity bombs, or B-52s armed with air-launched cruise missiles (ALCMs) or advanced cruise missiles (ACMs). Alternatives such as these, it is argued, would pose fewer problems than dual-capable aircraft in Europe. On operational grounds, intercontinental and/or sea-based systems would have less or no need for aerial refuelling, fighter escorts or suppression of enemy air defences. They would also probably be able to perform their missions with greater reliability. On political grounds, it is argued, relying on these systems would mean fewer complications over the use of Allied facilities and over Allies performing delivery functions.

The US would make every effort to consult with its Allies if it were ever obliged to consider using nuclear weapons in NATO's defence, even if no US weapons were present in Europe. The supposed advantage of avoiding consultation is thus politically implausible. The deeper flaw of this argument, however, is that it concentrates on military operational considerations and ignores the political and strategic functions of US nuclear weapons in Europe, such as the Alliance cohesion derived from sharing roles and responsibilities.

Could the UK's decision to abandon its air-delivered nuclear capability (WE-177 gravity bombs) and rely solely on *Trident* for sub-strategic missions nonetheless set an example that some might recommend for the US? All WE-177s were withdrawn from service in March 1998. Although the UK, in contrast to the US, never planned to provide any of its gravity bombs to Allies, some observers might cite the British example to question America's continued reliance on dual-capable aircraft and nuclear gravity bombs. It should be recognised, however, that the US has extended-deterrence commitments in Europe, and that its nuclear presence makes the transatlantic nuclear link manifest in programmes of cooperation with European allies. Air-delivered weapons (including those based in Europe under NATO auspices) give the US and NATO posture additional flexibility. One of the reasons why London felt able to abandon the WE-177s was that they did not have a role comparable to that of US weapons in promoting the sharing of responsibilities and maintaining the transatlantic link. It appears, moreover, that the British do not see *Trident* as NATO's sub-strategic 'weapon of choice'. London would expect any Alliance sub-strategic nuclear operations to involve a sharing of roles and responsibilities, including allied nuclear-capable aircraft as well as *Trident*.

Proponents of withdrawing US nuclear forces from Europe have advanced other arguments, including financial costs and safety and security. According to this view, it would be cheaper for the US (and for the Allies with nuclear-related responsibilities) to rely on other capabilities, such as TLAM-Ns or *Trident* SLBMs, for sub-strategic purposes. But this argument often fails to distinguish between the costs of maintaining or abandoning specific capabilities and the political and strategic consequences. The US nuclear presence in Europe is a relatively low-cost investment in Alliance security and US influence in international politics.

The expense of the US nuclear posture in Europe is low because the aircraft are dual-capable. As long as the US intends to keep fighter-bombers in Europe for conventional missions, the aircraft and their pilots, bomb-loading equipment, communications systems and associated infrastructure assets will have to be maintained anyway. Similarly, USAF training sorties with dual-capable aircraft are almost never wholly nuclear in nature, but almost always include conventional elements. The purely nuclear part of the US posture in Europe is mostly a 'sunk' investment – that is, the costs for the weapons, storage sites and associated equipment and infrastructure have already been incurred. These sites have been renovated and strengthened, and will require minimal maintenance expenditure for many years to come. Continuing costs mainly relate to the guards and custodial agents at storage sites.

The safety and security argument calls attention to the risk of an accident or terrorist incident that could undermine public support for Alliance policies. By definition, such an accident or incident could not befall a US nuclear weapon in Europe if all were withdrawn, and SLBMs and TLAM-Ns at sea are less vulnerable to terrorists than are nuclear-storage sites on land. The historical judgment in NATO has nonetheless been that the risks which the Alliance has accepted are reasonable, in view of the strategic and political benefits of maintaining a US nuclear presence, and substantial investments have been made to diminish these risks. Today's posture is accordingly even more secure than in the past, and involves a significantly smaller number of sites.

## US Strategic Nuclear Forces, START and Extended Deterrence

US strategic nuclear forces have been significant to America's allies in NATO since the founding of the Alliance. European officials and experts generally agree that one of the important functions of the US nuclear presence in Europe is to provide a link to the strategic forces constituting the ultimate deterrent to aggression or coercion. Ever since the Soviet Union launched *Sputnik* in 1957 and developed the world's first ICBMs, the Alliance has been subject to periodic crises of confidence. In essence, these have stemmed from European doubts about America's will to defend its allies, given the risk of prompt intercontinental nuclear retaliation from Russia. These doubts have been aggravated whenever Americans have expressed anxieties about US strategic capabilities. They did so during the 'bomber-gap' and 'missile-gap' controversies in the late 1950s and early 1960s and during the debates about the Strategic Arms

Limitation Talks (SALT) II Treaty, ICBM vulnerability and 'grey-area' systems of hypothetically intercontinental range, such as the *Backfire* bomber, in the late 1970s and early 1980s.

If a debate emerged in the US about the adequacy of the country's strategic-force posture for national security, allied experts and officials would probably ask questions about the implications for NATO, as well as for Japan and other beneficiaries of US nuclear guarantees. America's perceived commitment might matter more in reassuring allies than the size of the force and its specific characteristics. Short of a grave crisis in which the resolve and operational capabilities of the US would be tested, its strategic nuclear forces are significant for extended deterrence in Europe mainly on a political level.

Russian failure to ratify – and hence implement – START II is costly, both for Moscow and Washington. Under US law, America cannot reduce its forces below START I levels before Russia's ratification of START II. In February 1999, US Secretary of Defense William Cohen indicated that America could reduce its SSBN fleet to 14, eliminating four older submarines while retaining the capability to deploy a force at approximately START I levels. Some have suggested additional changes in strategic-force postures, notably in alert levels, as a complement to treaty-defined reductions in numerical ceilings and/or constraints on force composition. Some concepts for de-alerting strategic forces could harm extended deterrence. Measures such as separating warheads from delivery systems are usually advanced as prescriptions for safety against accidental or unauthorised launches. However, if de-alerting measures impaired readiness and made a large proportion of US forces more vulnerable to surprise or short-warning attacks, they could damage both strategic stability and extended deterrence. Concentrating warheads in a small number of storage sites could degrade crisis stability by creating lucrative targets.

## Theatre and National Missile Defence

Theatre missile defence (TMD) need not have a direct impact on the US nuclear presence in Europe. In the June 1994 framework document on WMD proliferation, the Allies agreed to 'improve defence capabilities of NATO and its members to protect NATO territory, populations and forces against WMD use'.[5] The Alliance's Senior

Defence Group on Proliferation devised an action plan, approved by Alliance Defence Ministers in June 1996, calling for 'extended air defences, including tactical ballistic missile defence for deployed forces', as one of the 'highest priority' tasks in dealing with the proliferation of WMD and associated delivery systems.[6]

Work on TMD is under way in several fora in NATO, including the Air Defence Committee. If the South Asian nuclear tests in 1998 mark a weakening of the non-proliferation regime and are seen as likely to augur an increased threat, the incentives for NATO governments to procure effective TMD capabilities may grow. NATO TMD and air defences are, however, unlikely to achieve such a high level of effectiveness that the need for nuclear-deterrent forces, including US weapons in Europe, would disappear. These forces and TMD are complementary capabilities.

Developments during 1998, including unexpected North Korean tests of long-range missiles, helped to change US policy on national missile defence (NMD). On 20 January 1999, Cohen announced plans to fund the deployment of an NMD system that would 'provide a limited defense for the fifty states against long-range missile threats posed by rogue nations'.

*theatre missile defence may become increasingly attractive*

Although Cohen emphasised that no deployment decision would be made until June 2000, the funds could support deployment in 2005. This approach, according to Cohen, is 'the optimal one to provide a capable NMD system as soon as possible'. Cohen stressed that the 'limited NMD capability' under development 'is focused primarily on countering rogue nation threats and will not be capable of countering Russia's nuclear deterrent'. While the 'NMD development program is being conducted consistent with the terms of the ABM [Anti-Ballistic Missile] Treaty', a deployed system 'may require modifications to the Treaty', and 'the Administration is working to determine the nature and scope of these modifications'.[7]

US NMD programmes implying a significant expansion of treaty-permitted defences or US withdrawal from the ABM Treaty could revive the European–American arguments that emerged in the mid-1980s over President Ronald Reagan's Strategic Defense Initiative (SDI). As in the SDI disputes, many European politicians, officials and experts would probably deplore American efforts to seek NMD. European critics of NMD would probably argue that, rather than increasing America's ability to offer credible guarantees to Allies, NMD would provoke confrontation with Russia, undermine strategic stability, hamper progress in US–Russian strategic nuclear-arms reductions, complicate the maintenance of the British and French deterrent forces, and create 'differing zones of security' within the Alliance.[8]

If the US decided to pursue NMD capabilities beyond the single site permitted by the ABM Treaty, and could not obtain Russian concurrence in the Treaty's corresponding revision, tension with Russia could lead Moscow to make threats against NATO Europe as well as the US. In effect, this could underscore NATO Europe's vulnerability in retaliation for any decrease in US national vulnerability. Complex results could follow: perceptions of an increased need by NATO's European members for US nuclear protection; a greater US ability to offer such protection, if national missile defences significantly reduced America's vulnerability to Russian nuclear retaliation; and annoyance in NATO Europe that the US had sought national defences beyond current ABM Treaty limits. However, it seems unlikely that US pursuit of NMD beyond current ABM Treaty limits would lead to outrage in NATO Europe jeopardising the very survival of the Alliance or the US nuclear presence in Europe. America's European Allies would be much more likely to press the US to limit any NMD deployments to activities acceptable to Russia, in view of their convictions about the requirements for strategic stability.

## The Debate over No-First-Use

There have been several signs of growing interest in no-first-use pledges in the US since the end of the Cold War. In 1992, Les Aspin, then Chairman of the House Armed Services Committee (he became Secretary of Defense in 1993) argued that a no-first-use policy could support US non-proliferation objectives. In Aspin's view, retaining a first-use option for NATO's security could 'undercut our non-proliferation efforts by legitimizing nuclear weapons and nuclear use'.[9] In 1995, three RAND analysts, David Gompert, Kenneth Watman and Dean Wilkening, called attention to apparent contradictions between US policy in NATO and US NSAs in the context of the NPT. They proposed that America adopt a no-first-use-of-WMD policy which would 'place adversaries on notice that the United States might use nuclear weapons in retaliation if American interests are attacked with weapons of mass destruction first. At the same time, the policy would pledge not to use nuclear weapons in response to a purely conventional attack'.[10]

US adoption of a no-first-use pledge could damage the Alliance in several ways. It would be contrary to the explicit policies of the UK and France. It would be inconsistent with the established policy assumptions of security élites in Europe's NATO members, who would see a no-first-use pledge as tantamount to offering a 'green light' to aggression by conventional, chemical or biological means. No-first-use could therefore undermine Alliance cohesion and security, and could even increase the risks of nuclear proliferation in and around NATO Europe.

British governments have repeatedly underlined their opposition to no-first-use pledges. In 1993, Malcolm Rifkind stated that 'The clear implication of any such declaration would be that conventional aggression could be undertaken without fear of crossing the nuclear threshold'.[11] German analysts close to traditional official thinking have been no less emphatic in underscoring the importance of first-use options for extended deterrence: 'Inseparably linked to the credibility of extended deterrence is the willingness to use nuclear weapons first; otherwise, one would signal to a potential opponent that one would rather accept conventional defeat than nuclear escalation'.[12] French officials and analysts have been almost unanimous in condemning no-first-use pledges. Pascal Boniface, for example, has dismissed them as 'unverifiable and incompatible with the very concept of deterrence'.[13] French analysts in particular have also scorned US concepts such as those advanced by Aspin for promoting non-proliferation by setting a 'good example' and 'delegitimising' the West's own nuclear forces. In 1993, Pierre Hassner declared:

*a no-first-use pledge could be damaging*

> *I do not believe at all that nuclear weapons have been delegitimised in the eyes of Pakistan, of Iran, of the various potential proliferators. I believe that the conventional idea according to which all that is because we are not setting the*

*right example is purely illusory. In my opinion, anyone who*
*believes that, if nuclear disarmament by the major Powers*
*went faster, that would dissuade Mr. Saddam Hussein or the*
*Governments of Iran or Pakistan from trying to procure*
*nuclear weapons would, as Dr Johnson said, believe*
*anything.*[14]

A no-first-use pledge could limit the contingencies in which
US nuclear forces in Europe would be relevant, and it could affect
Alliance cohesion and the willingness of European governments to
host these forces. It is widely agreed that 'purposeful ambiguity'
offers more for Alliance security than does no-first-use. Preserving
NATO's core function of collective defence, including US nuclear
commitments, has been seen by virtually all the Allies as a priority in
the review of the Strategic Concept. As the Dutch Ambassador to the
US, Joris Michael Vos, pointed out in February 1998, NATO's
'commitment to collective defense and the trans-Atlantic link, and
adherence to the nuclear [policy] paragraphs [in the 1991 Strategic
Concept], should be maintained. These represent the heart of the
organization, and changing them would alter NATO's essence and
purpose irrevocably'.[15] Canada and Germany are the only Alliance
governments to have suggested that changes in NATO's nuclear-
weapon policy might be warranted on non-proliferation grounds. In
December 1998, Canadian Foreign Minister Lloyd Axworthy told the
NAC that 'We should be circumspect about the political value we
place on NATO nuclear forces, lest we furnish arguments
proliferators can use to try to justify their own nuclear programs'.[16]
In October 1998, the SPD–Green coalition agreement declared that
the new German government would 'support the renunciation of
first-use policies'.[17]

There is little support for these views in other Alliance
governments. For the most part, the Allies uphold the 1991 Strategic
Concept principle that nuclear forces 'fulfill an essential role by
ensuring uncertainty in the mind of any aggressor about the nature
of the Allies' response to military aggression'.[18] By this logic, a no-
first-use pledge would undermine deterrence, including against
chemical and biological threats. It would also damage the non-
proliferation regime by implying a weakening of US security
commitments to the Allies. In December 1998, the German and

Canadian Defence Ministers joined with their counterparts in the
Defence Planning Committee and the NPG in a communiqué
reaffirming the principle outlined in the Strategic Concept.[19]

## Future US Policies

Future US policies regarding nuclear weapons are in some ways less
predictable than those of the other NPT-recognised nuclear powers.
The US may be more inclined to reduce the significance of nuclear
weapons in international politics because of the great sense of
security America currently enjoys. This stems in part from its
confidence in its preponderance of conventional military power. In
1992, then Secretary of Defense Dick Cheney declared that 'No
country is our match in conventional military technology and the
ability to apply it'.[20]

Since 1991, both Republican and Democrat administrations
have taken steps consistent with a 'marginalising' approach to
nuclear deterrence. The Bush administration decisions announced in
September 1991 and January 1992 are particularly noteworthy:
removing most of the remaining US nuclear presence in Europe;
removing nuclear-delivery systems from US aircraft carriers; ending
all programmes for new nuclear delivery systems (including the
small single-warhead ICBM and the
short-range attack missile (SRAM)-2     *the US 'lead*
and SRAM-T); and shortening the     *and hedge' policy*
ACM's production run. Clinton
administration officials have at times characterised the US approach,
notably with regard to START II, as a 'lead and hedge' policy:
seeking to 'lead' Russia and other nuclear-weapon states towards
lower levels of nuclear forces and improved safety and non-
proliferation measures, while retaining a 'hedge' of nuclear
capabilities and reconstitution assets as a precaution against
potential political setbacks and confrontations.[21] Depending on the
course of domestic and international developments, the US may take
further steps in the 'leading' direction in future years.

Questions have also been raised about America's staying-
power given domestic demands for national resources. The
disappearance of an obvious major threat to NATO has, for many
Americans, called into question the need to maintain much of the
remaining overseas military presence. In 1994 and 1995, the House of

Representatives approved amendments that called for reducing US
military personnel in NATO Europe to 25,000 unless the host nations
paid 75% of the non-personnel costs associated with this deployment. Advocates of these amendments all cited essentially economic
arguments: equity in burden-sharing, deficit reduction and economic
competitiveness.[22] It is not clear whether the votes on these
amendments should be interpreted as simply another instance of
Congressional criticism of Europeans over NATO burden-sharing, or
as evidence of a significant unravelling of the Euro-American
strategic consensus among US legislators. Neither amendment
resulted in actual legislation because neither won sufficient support
in the Senate.

Reducing the US military presence in Europe to 25,000 could
affect the remaining US nuclear presence there since military
personnel are responsible for safety and security at nuclear-storage
sites. Reductions in the US military presence in Europe after the end
of the Cold War (from 341,000 in 1989 to 109,000 in 1995) created
severe personnel constraints, encouraging the consolidation of
remaining nuclear weapons at a smaller number of bases.[23]

The Atlantic Alliance has historically enjoyed a high level of
approval and legitimacy in the US. The argument for continued
engagement is that US commitments are essential to sustain
collective-defence institutions.[24] The Clinton administration has
expressed its firm support for maintaining US nuclear forces and
commitments in Europe. In early 1998, Secretary of Defense Cohen
wrote that 'a credible Alliance nuclear posture continues to require
widespread participation by European allies in collective defense
planning for nuclear roles, peacetime basing of nuclear forces on
their territories, and command, control, and consultation arrangements'.[25]

The US Senate also sent a positive signal in April 1998
regarding continued US engagement in European security. In
consenting to the ratification of the protocols to the North Atlantic
Treaty for the accession of the Czech Republic, Hungary and Poland,
the Senate stipulated that the conditions 'binding upon the
President' would include respect for 'the core concepts contained in
the 1991 Strategic Concept of NATO'. Furthermore, the Senate
declared that the 'the upcoming revision of that document will

reflect' principles such as this reaffirmation of US nuclear commitments:

> *Nuclear weapons will continue to make an essential contribution to deterring aggression, especially aggression by potential adversaries armed with nuclear, biological, or chemical weapons. A credible NATO nuclear deterrent posture requires the stationing of United States nuclear forces in Europe, which provides an essential political and military link between Europe and North America, and the widespread participation of NATO members in nuclear roles. In addition, the NATO deterrent posture will continue to ensure uncertainty in the mind of any potential aggressor about the nature of the response by NATO members to military aggression.*[26]

This portion of the resolution of ratification, proposed by Republican Senator John Kyl, was approved by the Senate by 90 votes to nine, whereas the accession of the three new Allies was approved by 80 to 19.[27]

A tendency to question the usefulness of US alliances has nonetheless emerged since the end of the Cold War. Some prominent commentators have argued that the US should withdraw its extended-deterrence commitments because they are likely to expose America to unnecessary nuclear risks.[28] Referring to NATO enlargement, *New York Times* columnist Thomas L. Friedman has written, 'My daddy always said to me: "Son, never go into a global thermonuclear war to protect a country you can't find on the map"'.[29] In an interview in October 1995, Secretary of Defense Perry was asked what was so 'sacred' about NATO. He replied in terms of long-term regional stabilisation: 'There are still 20,000 nuclear weapons in the former Soviet Union. And the political and the economic recovery going on in those countries is extremely fragile ... So we have a very strong interest in the security and stability of Europe. NATO, in my judgment, is the linchpin of maintaining that stability'.[30]

These arguments are likely to strike some Americans as abstract speculation about what might happen in the distant future in regions that appear to be sufficiently peaceful or remote. They may not therefore be persuasive to those reluctant to accept the continuing obligations they imply. Some American politicians and commentators may ask whether lessening the long-term possibility of major-power regional rivalries and wars is worth the expense and security risks.

This paper argues that there is a strong case for the US to maintain nuclear forces and commitments in Europe and to continue working closely with NATO allies in developing and implementing nuclear policy. Nevertheless, many factors could affect decisions on whether the US nuclear presence is reduced, removed or retained. Variables that today appear scarcely worth mentioning could, in the long term, prove to be of profound importance. Factors which could lead to the reduction or removal of the US nuclear presence in Europe include:

- a 'delegitimisation' of nuclear deterrence through an accident or incident involving nuclear weapons, a confrontation raising the prospect of their operational use, or their actual operational use, perhaps in a region distant from NATO Europe, such as South Asia or the Middle East;
- arms-control negotiations and agreements with Russia;
- proposals to reassure the Russians and engage in 'confidence-building', notably in the context of NATO enlargement;
- arguments for saving money, reallocating personnel, avoiding safety and security risks, and concentrating exclusively on conventional missions with overseas-deployed forces by relying on off-shore and US-based nuclear weapons for deterrence;

- decreased threat perceptions, owing to Russia's successful democratisation and its cooperation in dealing with international security challenges, and/or political reform and the abandonment of WMD aspirations by suspected proliferants;
- increased US reluctance to accept extended-deterrence responsibilities, particularly in the context of NATO enlargement;
- no-first-use pledges;
- new nuclear-modernisation debates in a no-test environment;
- NATO's further evolution towards collective-security interventions in the former Yugoslavia and beyond, with less attention to the collective-defence tasks that help to justify US nuclear forces and commitments in Europe; and
- general reductions in the US military presence in Europe because of security priorities elsewhere, constraints on defence budgets or other reasons.

Many factors could confirm the need to maintain the US nuclear presence in Europe. These include:

- benefits to Alliance cohesion stemming from the widespread sharing of roles and responsibilities;
- increased threat perceptions, owing to a confrontational dictatorship or civil war in Russia, and/or the emergence of belligerent and well-armed WMD proliferants;
- increased emphasis on nuclear forces in Russia's diplomacy and military doctrine, in part due to deficiencies in the country's conventional military posture;
- Alliance judgments that balanced political and strategic relations between NATO and Russia require a US nuclear presence, even if Russia successfully democratises;
- US determination to retain a leading role in European security affairs;
- the widespread conviction in Europe's NATO members that no West European alternative to US nuclear forces and commitments is politically feasible or strategically credible;
- US acceptance of new extended-deterrence responsibilities through NATO enlargement;
- US concern about the risks inherent in a perceived dis-

engagement of America's commitments, including a higher probability of nuclear proliferation, new power competitions and the renationalisation of defence policies; and

- the risk of operational use of nuclear weapons, perhaps for decisive war-termination in a regional conflict unconnected with NATO.

This paper argues that US and Allied interests and risk assessments favour those factors which tend to confirm retaining US nuclear forces and commitments in Europe. Aside from general considerations, such as political stabilisation and Alliance cohesion, uncertainties in Russia and WMD-proliferation challenges are likely to support maintaining US nuclear forces and commitments in Europe in the next ten to 15 years, and beyond.

In each of the areas surveyed in this paper, pitfalls will have to be avoided if the Alliance's security interests are to be protected. Priorities are likely to remain deterrence and war-prevention, Alliance cohesion and security, political stabilisation in Europe and beyond, and non-proliferation. Some policy prescriptions – such as the US adopting a no-first-use pledge or a reconstitution approach to its nuclear posture in Europe – would almost certainly be counter-productive. Other policy challenges, such as NATO enlargement, West European nuclear cooperation and arms control, may present opportunities to enhance Alliance security if handled prudently.

Whether US nuclear capabilities and commitments in Europe will be sustained will depend, above all, on US discernment, determination and staying-power. The US is likely to be a central decision-maker in dealing with all the issues surveyed in this paper. The implications for NATO nuclear-consultation institutions and US nuclear commitments to European security will be a central consideration in the policy-making of most European members of NATO. US assessments and decisions will probably carry decisive weight within the Atlantic Alliance in areas such as arms control, WMD proliferation and analyses of developments in Russia.

If the US concluded that it remains in its interests – and in those of the Alliance as a whole – to maintain some US nuclear forces in Europe, the Allies would in all likelihood endorse that conclusion. If the US decided to withdraw its remaining nuclear presence and assert that its commitments could be honoured with off-shore and US-based capabilities, Europe's NATO governments would have little choice but to accept that decision. They would be obliged, once again, to redefine the requirements of extended deterrence in terms of what the US was prepared to make available.

Withdrawing all US nuclear forces from Europe would constitute a break without precedent in the history of NATO, and would reawaken long-standing European anxieties about the potential disengagement of US nuclear commitments. It could have far-reaching political effects, because European political–military establishments have been accustomed since the early 1950s to seeing a US nuclear presence in Europe as a proof of America's commitment. It is unclear how long – and with what credibility – the robustness of US nuclear commitments could be asserted without any nuclear presence in Europe.

The long-standing US position has been that, 'As the principal means by which Alliance members share nuclear risks and burdens, these aircraft and their [nuclear] weapons must be based in Europe'.¹ Relying solely on nuclear forces at sea and in the US would be unsatisfactory from the viewpoint of many Europeans and Americans. It would imply a lack of participation in nuclear roles by those Allies which are not nuclear-weapon states, and an Allied reluctance to identify with the nuclear posture and to demonstrate NATO's cohesion and resolve. The non-nuclear European countries that accept nuclear-basing and delivery roles and responsibilities would lose these tasks. Fewer European political–military élites would be well-informed about Alliance nuclear-weapon issues. Divisions between those states with nuclear weapons and those without would become more distinct in NATO, the WEU and the EU, damaging Western (and West European) political and strategic unity. Alliance cohesion could significantly diminish, while the prospects for transatlantic misunderstanding and mistrust would increase.

In the short term, political upheavals in Russia or in its relations with neighbouring states and nuclear proliferation in South Asia and beyond could reinforce the judgment that NATO must continue to maintain nuclear capabilities. The new South Asian situation could lead to various outcomes, including closer security ties between Russia and India and greater instability in India–

Pakistan and India–China relations. But it seems unlikely to provide any lasting or effective boost to endeavours to abolish nuclear weapons, much less efforts to bring about the complete and general disarmament envisaged in the NPT.

Threats to Alliance security that only nuclear weapons can parry or, at least, provide an insurance policy against, therefore seem likely to persist. While the specific characteristics of the Alliance's nuclear posture and associated command-and-control questions have intermittently become controversial issues, the Allies have consistently upheld US nuclear forces and commitments as essential elements of the transatlantic link. Given the historical pattern and entrenched nature of the conviction in NATO Europe that the US nuclear presence gives credibility to US commitments, it is doubtful whether other means to achieve this could be found. Withdrawing the remaining nuclear systems in Europe would therefore send a signal of disengagement and undermine the credibility of assurances that the US intends to remain committed to European security. It would be destabilising, with potentially serious long-term repercussions. It would eventually provoke debates and raise anxieties that are not now present. The withdrawal of a sense of US protection could create incentives for some European states to seek nuclear weapons, or to form coalitions to compensate for the apparent disengagement of US nuclear commitments. The sense that America was withdrawing from leadership responsibilities could stimulate competition for primacy among the larger European states.

The implications for US as well as general Western policy seem self-evident. No joint West European deterrent capable of acting as a substitute for US forces and commitments is on the horizon. US nuclear commitments provide an important element of structural stability that enhances prospects for progress in democratisation and economic development and the pursuit of constructive relations among the major powers. It remains in US and Western interests for the US to maintain the credibility of its nuclear commitments with a continuing nuclear-weapon presence on the territory of European NATO Allies, and to engage its allies in nuclear consultation and planning.

*notes*

## Acknowledgments

This paper draws on two earlier works: 'Europe and Nuclear Deterrence', *Survival*, vol. 35, no. 3, Autumn 1993, pp. 97–120; and *US Nuclear Weapons in Europe: Prospects and Priorities*, Future Roles Series Paper 7 (Livermore, CA: Sandia National Laboratories, December 1996). The author would like to thank the following for their comments on earlier drafts of this paper: Peppino DeBiaso, Frank Dellermann, Thérèse Delpech, Christopher Donnelly, Sadi Erguvenc, Mark Etherton, Patrick Garrity, François Géré, Karinne Gordon, Philip Gordon, Sidney Graybeal, John Harvey, François Heisbourg, David Honeywell, Bruce Ianacone, Fred Iklé, Robert Irvine, Mark Jackson, William Kahn, Karl-Heinz Kamp, Mustafa Kibaroglu, Jacob Kipp, Joachim Krause, Stephen Lambert, Steven Maaranen, Mark Maguire, Andrew Mathewson, Winfried Mertens, Keith Payne, Joseph Pilat, Robert Rinne, Michael Rühle, Diego Ruiz Palmer, Peter Ryan, Gregory Schulte, Duygu Bazoglu Sezer, Richard Shearer, James Sherr, David Shilling, Bernard Sitt, Bruno Tertrais, Stephen Willmer, Ian Woodman and Roberto Zadra.

## Introduction

1 See, for example, 'Strategic Concept for the Defense of the North Atlantic Area', approved on 1 December 1949, in US Department of State, *Foreign Relations of the United States, 1949, Western Europe* (Washington DC: US Government Printing Office (USGPO), 1975), vol. 4, pp. 352–58.
2 For the lower number, see Robert S. Norris and William M. Arkin, 'US Nuclear Weapon Locations', *Bulletin of the Atomic Scientists*, November–December 1995, pp. 74–75. For the higher, see Alan Riding, 'NATO Will Cut Atom Weapons for Aircraft Use', *New York Times*, 18 October 1991, p. A1.
3 *Enhancing Alliance Collective Security: Shared Roles, Risks and Responsibilities in the Alliance, A*

*Report by NATO's Defence Planning Committee*, December 1988, paragraph 36. The UK provided its own nuclear gravity bombs for aircraft use; the last British bombs – WE-177s – were withdrawn from service in March 1998.
4 North Atlantic Council (NAC), 'Strategic Concept', 7 November 1991, paragraph 56, available in *NATO Handbook* (Brussels: NATO Office of Information and Press, October 1995), pp. 235–48.
5 David S. Yost, 'The History of NATO Theater Nuclear Force Policy: Key Findings from the Sandia Conference', *Journal of Strategic Studies*, vol. 15, no. 2, June 1992, pp. 228–61.

**Chapter 1**

1 NAC, 'Strategic Concept', 7 November 1991, paragraph 21.
2 *Ibid.*, paragraph 14.
3 *Ibid.*, paragraphs 55, 57.
4 John Deutch, Deputy Secretary of Defense, comments at press conference, news release by the Office of the Assistant Secretary of Defense for Public Affairs, 22 September 1994, p. 7.
5 See C. J. Dick, *The Russian Army: Present Plight and Future Prospects*, Occasional Brief 31 (Camberley: Conflict Studies Research Centre, November 1994); and M. J. Orr, *The Current State of the Russian Armed Forces* (Camberley: Conflict Studies Research Centre, November 1996).
6 See, for example, Lothar Rühl, 'Offensive Defence in the Warsaw Pact', *Survival*, vol. 33, no. 5, September–October 1991, pp. 442–50.
7 Igor Rodionov, cited in Mary C. FitzGerald, 'Chief of Russia's General Staff Academy Speaks Out on Moscow's New Military Doctrine', *Orbis*, vol. 37, no. 2, Spring 1993, p. 288.
8 'Russian Federation National Security Blueprint', approved by Russian Federation Presidential Edict No. 1,300, 17 December 1997, *Rossiyskaya Gazeta*, 26 December 1997, in Foreign Broadcast Information Service (FBIS), *Daily Report*, SOV-97-364, 30 December 1997, pp. 9, 16.
9 'Kremlin Approves Major Defense Policy Document', *Jamestown Foundation Monitor*, vol. 4, no. 149, 4 August 1998, p. 1.
10 Yevgeny Primakov, interview on Russian television, 24 May 1997, quoted in Mitchell Landsberg, 'Russia Adopts 1st Strike Policy', *Associated Press*, 25 May 1997; and Ivan Rybkin, quoted in 'Rybkin's Remarks on First Strike "Hypothetical"', *Rossiyskaya Gazeta*, 11 February 1997, in FBIS, *Daily Report*, TAC-97-007, 11 February 1997. Among the many statements by Russian military authors, see V. V. Starukhin and Gennady A. Kuznetsov, 'The Basis of Strategic Stability: It Depends On a Balance of Comparable Nuclear Threats', *Nezavisimoye Voyennoye Obozreniye*, no. 31, 22 August 1997, p. 6, in FBIS, *Daily Report*, FBIS-TAC-97-239, 27 August 1997; and V. V. Kruglov and M. Ye. Sosnovsky, 'On the Role of Nonstrategic Nuclear Weapons in Nuclear Deterrence', *Voyennaya Mysl*, no. 6, September 1997, pp. 11–14, in FBIS, *Daily Report*, 5 December 1997.
11 Rodionov, quoted in Mary C. FitzGerald, 'The Russian Image of Future War', *Comparative Strategy*, vol. 13, no. 2, April–June 1994, p. 173.
12 Viktor Mikhailov, Igor

Andryushin and Alexander Chernyshov, 'NATO's Expansion and Russia's Security', *Vek*, 20 September 1996, available at *RIA Novosti*, www.rian.ru.

[13] Bill Gertz, 'Perry Cites Evidence of Russian Nuke Test', *Washington Times*, 8 March 1996, p. 18.

[14] William Drozdiak, 'The Next Step for NATO: Handling Russia', *Washington Post National Weekly Edition*, 11 May 1998, p. 15.

[15] Alastair Macdonald, 'Russia: Yeltsin Wins Praise, Scorn at Home over NATO Deal', *Reuters Textline*, 28 May 1997.

[16] Thomas W. Lippman, 'Slow Going for Arms Control', *Washington Post National Weekly Edition*, 29 January 1996, pp. 16–17.

[17] Paul Felgengauer, 'The Russian Army and the East–West Military Balance: Self-Deception and Mutual Misunderstanding Did Not End with the Cold War', *Segodnya*, 18 August 1995; extracts published in *The National Interest*, no. 42, Winter 1995–96, p. 116.

[18] Bruce G. Blair, 'Russian Control of Nuclear Weapons', in George Quester (ed.), *The Nuclear Challenge in Russia and the New States of Eurasia* (Armonk, NY and London: M. E. Sharpe, 1995), pp. 60–61.

[19] Sergey Rogov, quoted in Theresa Hitchens and Anton Zhigulsky, 'Hard-Line Russians Tout Nukes to Match West', *Defense News*, 20–26 November 1995, pp. 1, 36.

[20] Lev Rokhlin, quoted in 'Duma Defence Committee Chairman on Threat Posed by Army's Plight', *Argumenty i Fakty*, January 1997, in *Reuters Textline*, 18 January 1997.

[21] Deborah Yarsike Ball, 'The Unreliability of the Russian Officer Corps: Reluctant Domestic Warriors', in Kathleen C. Bailey and M. Elaine Price (eds), *Director's Series on Proliferation* (Livermore, CA: Lawrence Livermore National Laboratory, November 1995), p. 29.

[22] Jim Wolf, 'CIA Rates "Low" the Risk of Unauthorized Use of Russian Nuclear Warheads', *Washington Post*, 23 October 1996, p. A6.

[23] Vladimir Shlapentokh, 'Russia: Privatization and Illegalization of Social and Political Life', *Washington Quarterly*, vol. 19, no. 1, Winter 1996, p. 84.

[24] *Study on NATO Enlargement* (Brussels: NATO, September 1995), paragraph 58.

[25] 'Final Communiqué of the North Atlantic Council', 10 December 1996, paragraph 5.

[26] 'Founding Act on Mutual Relations, Cooperation and Security between the North Atlantic Treaty Organization and the Russian Federation', Paris, 27 May 1997, p. 7.

[27] Boris Yeltsin, quoted in Richard Balmforth, 'Russia: Yeltsin Attacks NATO over US Nukes in Europe', *Reuters*, 20 April 1996.

[28] Viktor Mikhailov, quoted in Lee Hockstader, 'Russia Warns of Attack if NATO Expands East', *Washington Post*, 16 February 1996, p. 29.

[29] Yevgeny Primakov, quoted in Thomas L. Friedman, 'Russia's NATO Fax', *New York Times*, 24 July 1996, p. A15.

[30] Mikhailov, Andryushin and Chernyshov, 'NATO's Expansion'.

[31] 'Special Institute Staff Suggests Russia Oppose NATO and the USA', Defence Research Institute, Moscow, October 1995, reproduced in English by the Conflict Studies Research Centre, Royal Military Academy, Sandhurst, April 1996, pp. 3, 5–7. This is a translation of a widely discussed article by Anton

Surikov which appeared in *Segodnya*, 20 October 1995.

[32] Anton Surikov, 'Some Aspects of Russian Armed Forces Reform', *European Security*, vol. 6, no. 3, Autumn 1997, p. 55.

[33] Paul Felgengauer, 'Russian Generals Aren't Interested in NATO Countries' Good Intentions', *Segodnya*, 23 June 1996, in *Current Digest of the Post-Soviet Press*, 19 July 1996, p. 31.


**Chapter 2**

[1] Walter B. Slocombe, 'The Future of US Nuclear Weapons in a Restructured World', in Patrick J. Garrity and Steven A. Maarenen (eds), *Nuclear Weapons in the Changing World: Perspectives from Europe, Asia, and North America* (New York: Plenum, 1992), p. 63.

[2] Mark N. Gose, 'The New Germany and Nuclear Weapons: Options for the Future', *Airpower Journal*, vol. 10, Special Edition, 1996, pp. 67–78.

[3] *Ibid.*, pp. 75, 78.

[4] Duygu Bazoglu Sezer, 'Turkey's New Security Environment, Nuclear Weapons and Proliferation', *Comparative Strategy*, vol. 14, no. 2, April–June 1995, p. 166.

[5] *Ibid.*, pp. 167–68.

[6] Mustafa Kibaroglu, 'Turkey's Quest for Peaceful Nuclear Power', *Nonproliferation Review*, vol. 4, no. 3, Spring–Summer 1997, pp. 41, 43.

[7] Volker Rühe cited in Michael Evans, 'NATO Says Farewell to Nuclear Conflict', *The Times*, 21 October 1992.

[8] Gregory L. Schulte, 'Responding to Proliferation – NATO's Role', *NATO Review*, no. 4, July 1995,

p. 15.

[9] *Ibid.*, pp. 18–19.

[10] 'Final Communiqué of the Defence Planning Committee and the Nuclear Planning Group', 13 June 1996, paragraph 6.

[11] Secretary of Defense William Perry, remarks at the Air War College conference 'Nuclear Proliferation Issues', Maxwell Air Force Base, AL, 26 April 1996.

[12] Robert Bell, quoted in R. Jeffrey Smith, 'Clinton Directive Changes Strategy On Nuclear Arms', *Washington Post*, 7 December 1997, p. A1.

[13] Ashton B. Carter and David B. Omand, 'Countering the Proliferation Risks: Adapting the Alliance to the New Security Environment', *NATO Review*, no. 5, September 1996, p. 13.

[14] Richard Dittbenner, 'Letter to the Editor', *Defense News*, 22–28 July 1996, p. 14.

[15] Michael Rühle, 'NATO and the Coming Proliferation Threat', *Comparative Strategy*, vol. 13, no. 3, July–September 1994, pp. 317–18.

[16] 'Special Institute Staff Suggests Russia Oppose NATO and the USA', p. 7.

[17] See R. Adam Moody, 'The Indian–Russian Light Water Reactor Deal', *Nonproliferation Review*, vol. 5, no. 1, Autumn 1997, pp. 112–22; and Howard Diamond, 'Russia, India Move Forward With Deals on Arms, Nuclear Power', *Arms Control Today*, June–July 1998, p. 25.


**Chapter 3**

[1] Jacques Chirac, speech at the Institut des Hautes Etudes de Défense Nationale, Paris, 8 June 1996, p. 6.

[2] 'Joint Statement by President Jacques Chirac and Prime Minister John Major', 29–30 October 1995.

[3] Alain Juppé, speech at the Institut des Hautes Etudes de Défense Nationale, 7 September 1995, pp. 3–5.

[4] 'Concept Commun Franco-Allemand en Matière de Sécurité et de Défense', *Le Monde*, 30 January 1997, p. 12.

[5] 'Interview de M. Jacques Chirac, Président de la République, Accordée au Magazine Allemand *Focus*, Palais de l'Élysée', 15 September 1997, p. 13; and speech by Prime Minister Lionel Jospin, Institut des Hautes Etudes de Défense Nationale, 4 September 1997, p. 4.

[6] Speech by Malcolm Rifkind, Paris, 30 September 1992, pp. 16–17.

[7] Comments by Malcolm Rifkind, press conference, 10 September 1995. See also interview with Prime Minister John Major, *Le Monde*, 29–30 October 1995.

[8] Volker Rühe and Karl Lamers quoted in Lorraine Millot, 'Foudre Allemande sur le Parapluie Français', *Libération*, 15 September 1995.

[9] See Josef Joffe, 'Atomschirm für Bonn? – "Wir Würden Lügen"', *Süddeutsche Zeitung*, 9–10 September 1995, p. 4.

[10] See comments by Hubert Védrine, in 'La Politique Etrangère de la France de 1981 à 1995', *Relations Internationales et Stratégiques*, no. 24, Winter 1996, pp. 24–25.

[11] Christoph Bertram, 'Britain's Nuclear Weapons and West German Security', in Karl Kaiser and John Roper (eds), *British–German Defence Cooperation: Partners within the Alliance* (London: Jane's, 1988), p. 209.

[12] Karl-Heinz Kamp, 'European Nuclear Cooperation: Prospects and Problems', presentation to the NATO NPG Staff Group Symposium, 3 March 1996, p. 7.

## Chapter 4

[1] *Report of the Canberra Commission on the Elimination of Nuclear Weapons* (Canberra: Canberra Commission on the Elimination of Nuclear Weapons, August 1996), Executive Summary, p. 2.

[2] 'Statement on Nuclear Weapons by International Generals and Admirals', 5 December 1996, reproduced in advertisement sponsored by the State of the World Forum, *Washington Post*, 6 December 1996, p. A41.

[3] 'Communiqué of the International Court of Justice', no. 96/23, 8 July 1996.

[4] According to Article VI of the Non-Proliferation Treaty (NPT), 'Each of the Parties to the Treaty undertakes to pursue negotiations in good faith on effective measures relating to cessation of the nuclear arms race at an early date and to nuclear disarmament, and on a treaty on general and complete disarmament under strict and effective international control'.

[5] White House Press Statement, 4 December 1996, cited in Craig Cerniello, 'Retired Generals Re-ignite Debate Over Abolition of Nuclear Weapons', *Arms Control Today*, vol. 26, no. 9, November–December 1996, p. 14.

[6] 'Communiqué of the International Court of Justice'.

[7] *Ibid*.

[8] See, for example, statement by unnamed British Foreign Office spokesman, in Christopher

Lockwood, 'Nuclear Arms Are Illegal, Court Rules', *Daily Telegraph*, 9 July 1996; statement by US State Department spokesman Nicholas Burns, in 'US Welcomes World Court's Refusal to Rule on Nukes', *Kyodo News Service*, 9 July 1996; and French Ministry of Foreign Affairs communiqué, 8 July 1996, in *Documents d'Actualité Internationale*, no. 17, 1 September 1996, p. 697.

[9] Walter B. Slocombe, statement before the Senate Governmental Affairs Subcommittee on International Security, Proliferation and Federal Services, Hearing on Nuclear Weapons and Deterrence, 12 February 1997, pp. 2, 5.

[10] *Report of the Canberra Commission*, p. 1.

[11] Slocombe, statement before the Senate Governmental Affairs Subcommittee on International Security, p. 6.

[12] Helmut Kohl, quoted in Ronald D. Asmus, *German Strategy and Opinion After the Wall, 1990–1993* (Santa Monica, CA: RAND, 1994), pp. 3–4.

[13] See David S. Yost, 'The Delegitimization of Nuclear Deterrence?', *Armed Forces and Society*, vol. 16, no. 4, Summer 1990, pp. 487–508.

[14] Merrill Walters, 'Responses', in Paul Leventhal and Yonah Alexander (eds), *Nuclear Terrorism: Defining the Threat* (Washington DC: Pergamon-Brassey's, 1986), p. 68.

[15] Joachim Krause, 'Proliferation Risks and their Strategic Relevance: What Role for NATO?', *Survival*, vol. 37, no. 2, Summer 1995, p. 147.

[16] 'Gorbachev's Remarks on Nuclear Arms Cuts', *New York Times*, 6 October 1991, p. 11.

[17] Interview with Russian Defence Minister Pavel Grachev, *Radio Moscow International*, 9 September 1994, in *BBC Summary of World Broadcasts, The Former USSR* (SWB/SU) 2099/S1, 13 September 1994.

[18] John Deutch, comments at a press conference, news release by the Office of the Assistant Secretary of Defense for Public Affairs, 22 September 1994, pp. 5–6, 12.

[19] 'US–Russian Joint Statement on Parameters on Future Reductions in Nuclear Forces', Helsinki, 21 March 1997.

[20] See, for example, statement by Victor Reis, Assistant Secretary for Defense Programs, US Department of Energy, before the House National Security Committee, Subcommittee on Military Procurement, 12 March 1996, p. 8.

[21] See Amy F. Woolf and Kara Wilson, *Russia's Nuclear Forces: Doctrine and Force Structure Issues* (Washington DC: Congressional Research Service (CRS), May 1997), p. 9.

[22] Slocombe, statement before the Senate Governmental Affairs Subcommittee on International Security, p. 4.

[23] Edward L. Warner III, statement before the Strategic Forces Subcommittee, Senate Armed Services Committee, Hearing on Nuclear Deterrence, 31 March 1998, p. 4.

[24] Speech by Alain Richard, Institut des Hautes Etudes de Défense Nationale, 10 February 1998, p. 5. Richard's estimate of Russian non-strategic nuclear warheads is exceptionally high.

[25] 'Final Communiqué, Ministerial Meetings of the Defence Planning Committee and the Nuclear

Planning Group', 17 December 1996, paragraph 9.

[26] 'Fact Sheet: Comprehensive Test Ban Treaty Safeguards', Office of the Press Secretary, The White House, 11 August 1995.

[27] Yurii Baturin, quoted in Open Media Research Institute (OMRI), *Daily Digest*, 19 April 1996.

[28] Gennady Udovenko, interview in *Post-Postup* (Lvov), 10–18 August 1996, in FBIS, *Daily Report*, SOV-96-161, 18 August 1996.

[29] 'Statement by the Delegations of Bulgaria, Croatia, the Czech Republic, Hungary, Poland, Romania, Slovakia and Slovenia to the Preparatory Committee for the 2000 Review Conference of the Parties to the Treaty on the Non-Proliferation of Nuclear Weapons', Geneva, 6 May 1998, NPT/CONF.2000/PC.II/24.

[30] Seth Faison, 'China Sets Off Nuclear Test, then Announces Moratorium', *New York Times*, 30 July 1996, p. A3.

[31] See, for example, Les Aspin, 'From Deterrence to Denuking: Dealing with Proliferation in the 1990s', House Armed Services Committee, 18 February 1992, p. 15.

[32] Greenpeace spokesman Hans Kristensen quoted in Andrew Marshall, 'Spirit of Treaty "Is Being Broken"', *The Independent*, 19 April 1995, p. 10. This issue was considered by the Allies before they adhered to the NPT. According to US Secretary of State Dean Rusk's report on the NPT to President Lyndon Johnson on 2 July 1968, the Treaty 'does not deal with arrangements for deployment of nuclear weapons within allied territory as these do not involve any transfer of nuclear weapons or control over them unless and until a decision were made to go to war, at which time the treaty would no longer be controlling'. See US Arms Control and Disarmament Agency, *Documents on Disarmament, 1968* (Washington DC: USGPO, 1969), p. 478. This issue was not prominent until 1995, when Greenpeace and other organisations drew attention to it. Several European NATO Allies, including Germany, explicitly rejected the interpretation of the NPT advanced by Greenpeace and others.

[33] 'Principles and Objectives for Nuclear Non-Proliferation and Disarmament', 11 May 1995, NPT/CONF.1995/32/DEC.2, Annex 2.

[34] See statement by Ambassador Arundhati Ghose, India's Permanent Representative to the Conference on Disarmament, Geneva, 20 June 1996.

[35] 'Canada and the Nuclear Challenge: Reducing the Political Value of Nuclear Weapons for the Twenty-First Century', *Report of the Standing Committee on Foreign Affairs and International Trade* (Ottawa: House of Commons, December 1998), p. 91.

**Chapter 5**

[1] 'Final Communiqué of the Defence Planning Committee and the Nuclear Planning Group', 13 June 1996, paragraph 8.

[2] For a discussion sympathetic to a reconstitution approach to nuclear deterrence in Europe, see Karl Kaiser, 'From Nuclear Deterrence to Graduated Conflict Control', *Survival*, vol. 32, no. 6, November–December 1990, pp. 483–96.

[3] Carlo Jean, 'The New European Strategic Environment',

*International Spectator*, vol. 26, January–March 1991, p. 56.
[4] David Omand, 'Nuclear Deterrence in a Changing World: The View from a UK Perspective', *RUSI Journal*, vol. 141, no. 3, June 1996, p. 17.
[5] 'Alliance Policy Framework on Proliferation of Weapons of Mass Destruction', Ministerial Meeting of the North Atlantic Council, Istanbul, 9 June 1994, paragraph 13.
[6] Carter and Omand, 'Countering the Proliferation Risks', p. 14.
[7] 'Statement by Secretary of Defense William Cohen on NMD and TMD Program Initiatives', Office of the Assistant Secretary of Defense (Public Affairs), 20 January 1999.
[8] See David S. Yost, 'Western Europe and the US Strategic Defense Initiative', *Journal of International Affairs*, vol. 41, no. 2, Summer 1988, pp. 269–323.
[9] Aspin, 'From Deterrence to Denuking', pp. 15–16.
[10] David Gompert, Kenneth Watman and Dean Wilkening, 'Nuclear First Use Revisited', *Survival*, vol. 37, no. 3, Autumn 1995, p. 27.
[11] Speech by Malcolm Rifkind, King's College London, 16 November 1993, p. 5.
[12] Thomas Enders, Holger H. Mey, and Michael Rühle, 'The New Germany and Nuclear Weapons', in Garrity and Maaranen (eds), *Nuclear Weapons in the Changing World*, p. 136.
[13] Pascal Boniface, 'La Dissuasion Peut se Passer des Essais Nucléaires', *Libération*, 9 March 1993.
[14] Pierre Hassner, 'Responses', in Serge Sur (ed.), *Nuclear Deterrence: Problems and Perspectives in the*

*1990s* (New York and Geneva: UN Institute for Disarmament Research, 1993), p. 158.
[15] Joris Michael Vos, quoted in Lisa Burgess, 'Nuclear Policy Battle Looms as NATO Expansion Nears', *Defense News*, 30 March 1998, p. 42.
[16] Lloyd Axworthy, address to the North Atlantic Council (NAC), Brussels, 8 December 1998.
[17] 'Aufbruch und Erneuerung – Deutschlands Weg ins 21. Jahrhundert', Koalitions-vereinbarung zwischen der Sozialdemokratischen Partei Deutschlands und Bündnis 90/Die Grünen, Bonn, 20 October 1998, paragraph 6.
[18] NAC, 'Strategic Concept', 7 November 1991, paragraph 55.
[19] 'Final Communiqué of the Ministerial Meeting of the Defence Planning Committee and the Nuclear Planning Group', 17 December 1998, paragraph 9.
[20] Dick Cheney, *Annual Report of the Secretary of Defense to the President and the Congress* (Washington DC: USGPO, February 1992), p. vi.
[21] See Stephen A. Cambone and Patrick J. Garrity, 'The Future of US Nuclear Policy', *Survival*, vol. 36, no 4, Winter 1994–95, pp. 73–95.
[22] *Congressional Record* (Washington DC: USGPO, 19 May 1994), pp. H3736–H3746; and *ibid.*, 14 June 1995, pp. H5955–H5962.
[23] See *NATO Nuclear Bases: US Should Seek Needs Reassessment and Increased Alliance Contributions*, Report to the Chairman, Subcommittee on Readiness, Committee on Armed Services, House of Representatives, GAO-NSIAD-94-84 (Washington DC: US General Accounting Office, December 1993), p. 4.

[24] See David S. Yost, *NATO Transformed: The Alliance's New Roles in International Security* (Washington DC: US Institute of Peace Press, 1998).
[25] William S. Cohen, *Annual Report of the Secretary of Defense to the President and the Congress* (Washington DC: USGPO, 1998), p. 7.
[26] 'Resolution of Ratification to the Protocols to the North Atlantic Treaty of 1949 on the Accession of Poland, Hungary, and the Czech Republic', 30 April 1998, in *Congressional Record*, 4 May 1998, pp. S4218–S4219.
[27] For the Senate's 90–9 approval of the Kyl amendment, see *Congressional Record*, 28 April 1998, p. S3698. For Senator Kyl's proposal of the amendment, see *Congressional Record*, 27 April 1998, p. S3624.
[28] Ted Galen Carpenter, 'Closing the Nuclear Umbrella', *Foreign Affairs*, vol. 73, no. 2, March–April 1994, pp. 8–13.
[29] Thomas L. Friedman, 'Porgy, Bess and NATO', *New York Times*, 9 April 1995, p. E15.
[30] William Perry, quoted in Elaine Sciolino, 'Soldiering On, Without an Enemy', *ibid.*, 29 October 1995, section 4, p. 4.

## Conclusion

[1] The White House, *National Security Strategy of the United States* (Washington DC: US GPO, August 1991), p. 26.